Brent Ruggles

What Do You Mean
I Can't Write?

WHAT DO YOU MEAN I CAN'T WRITE?

John S. Fielden
Ronald E. Dulek

Prentice-Hall, Inc., Englewood Cliffs, New Jersey

Prentice-Hall International, Inc., *London*
Prentice-Hall of Australia, Pty. Ltd., *Sydney*
Prentice-Hall Canada, Inc., *Toronto*
Prentice-Hall of India Private Ltd., *New Delhi*
Prentice-Hall of Japan, Inc., *Tokyo*
Prentice-Hall of Southeast Asia Pte. Ltd., *Singapore*
Whitehall Books, Ltd., Wellington, *New Zealand*
Editora Prentice-Hall do Brasil Ltda., *Rio de Janeiro*

© 1984 by

PRENTICE-HALL, INC.

Englewood Cliffs, N.J.

All rights reserved. No part of this
book may be reproduced in any form or
by any means, without permission in
writing from the publisher.

Library of Congress Cataloging in Publication Data

Fielden, John S.
  "What do you mean I can't write?"

  Includes index.
  1. English language—Business English.   2. Commercial
correspondence.   3. English language—Self-instruction.
I. Dulek, Ronald E.   II. Title.
PE1115.F484 1984   808'.066651   83-19207
ISBN 0-13-952028-7

Printed in the United States of America

THE AUTHORS

John S. Fielden, Ph.D., University Professor of Management Communications, University of Alabama, is the author of nine *Harvard Business Review* articles, including the all-time *Harvard Business Review Classic,* "What Do You Mean I Can't Write?" A consultant to IBM since 1964, Dr. Fielden is formerly Dean of the Business Schools of Boston University and the University of Alabama. He is a writing consultant to General Electric, Dun and Bradstreet, General Foods and other U.S. and Canadian firms.

Ronald E. Dulek, Ph.D., is Associate Professor and Coordinator of Management Communications at the University of Alabama. He is consultant to IBM, OSHA, the United States Department of Health and Human Services, AT&T, and other public and private organizations. His articles on business communications have been published in *Business Horizons, Journal of Business Communications, Personnel Journal, Personnel* magazine, and *IEEE Transactions on Professional Communications.*

DEDICATION

To Jean and Sally

ACKNOWLEDGMENTS

We wish to acknowledge the valuable contributions made to the development of materials in this book by Mr. Earnest B. Mercer of International Business Machines Corporation.

WRITE WELL
TO DO WELL

Why can't most people write as easily and effectively as they'd like? Because no one has taught them *how to!* Time after time in classes we conduct for large corporations and government agencies, we find participants sitting, biting their pencils in agony, trying to determine how to begin a letter assignment.

We pick one class member and ask him or her, "What are you trying to accomplish?" "Well," the answer goes, "right now I am trying to figure out what my first few words ought to be."

"That's not what we asked," we continue. "What are you trying to accomplish?"

"Well, you see, I want Mr. Jones to give me a chance to present my sales proposal."

"Oh! Suppose Mr. Jones were standing right here? What would you say to him then?"

"I'd say, 'I really would appreciate it if you would give me an opportunity to tell you how the product I represent would really help your organization.'"

"That sounds like a very good beginning," we respond. "Why don't you say just that?"

5

In our programs we feel as if we are frequently freeing people from a bondage of insecurity bred by their educational experiences. We find business people all tied up by concerns about whether they should or shouldn't split infinitives, or end sentences with prepositions, or repeat the same word more than twice in the same letter, even though each of these bugaboos has been denounced as nonsense by most knowledgeable experts.

In this book we unabashedly pose as experts. We make this statement because that is what *you want* us to be. Practical business people don't want to know various opinions as to whether one may use a perfectly harmless and idiomatic word as "hopefully." All business people want is to have someone knowledgeable sort out what is important for them to know—and then to tell them.

We take this approach to grammar, as you will see, in the following pages. We know you have been exposed to 300-page grammar books all your life. And we suspect, if you're typical of most business people, that you still feel pretty shaky about grammar. So we have thrown out all the grammatical quibbles and have reduced grammar to a very few simple rules which, when mastered by you, will enable you to avoid about 90 percent of the grammatical errors that a business person could make.

The focus of this book is primarily on how you *personally* can write better. It also offers advice from time to time on how you can do a much better job of managing, demanding, and obtaining good writing from others, if such is, or will be, your job.

The single greatest benefit you will get from the experience of reading "What Do You Mean I Can't Write?" will be the mastery of a critical vocabulary so necessary to being able to discuss business writing. Most people simply do not have the words with which to describe to another person what is good or bad about a given piece of business writing.

In our training classes, we display on a screen a series of good and bad business letters. We ask the class members whether they like each letter. They generally like the good letters and don't like the bad ones. But when we ask them to tell us *why* they like a letter or why they don't, they are tongue-tied. Why? They have no common critical vocabulary.

What you will definitely get from *What Do You Mean I Can't Write?* is a vocabulary which will enable you to articulate what is good and bad about a piece of writing. And in the process you will develop standards of excellence which from that point forward you will try to adhere to in every piece of on-the-job writing you do.

John S. Fielden
Ronald E. Dulek

We have made every effort to avoid sexist language in this text. In situations where a designation is necessary, such as in various scenarios, we have alternated male and female names.

CONTENTS

1

THE KEY TO SUCCESS: EFFECTIVE MANAGEMENT OF YOUR OWN AND OTHERS' WRITING

In many (if not most) offices, writing involves more than one person. One prepares the draft of a memo or report, and the other (especially if the communication is important) inspects and approves it. Teamwork between writers and their bosses can be effective only if both parties share a common critical vocabulary.

Unfortunately, that is seldom the case. At this very moment, somewhere in your company, some boss (call him Mr. Brown) is reading with dismay a draft of a letter written for his signature. He calls his assistant in and says, "Green, this is terrible. Take this letter back and do it over." Poor Green retires to revise the epistle. After he returns with the revision, Brown reads it with tightened lips: "This is worse than the first one! Do it over again!" Green, knees trembling, dashes off to give it one more try and ultimately returns with the final version. Mr. Brown reads it, slams it down, and states emphatically, "You simply can't write, Green! I'll have to do this myself!"

So he goes into his office, closes the door, pulls the drapes, dims the light, hunches over Green's draft, and revises it. The manager sends the edited version to word processing, and off it goes to the addressee. Poor Green, however, never sees it again. Moreover, Green has never learned what Brown didn't like about the letter.

In American industry this travesty passes for *management development*. And this in *the* most important area affecting Green's future!

It's incredible but true. But only in the area of written communication. If the boss took Green off to make an oral sales presentation to a customer, and Green butchered the presentation, the boss would be able to tell Green, point by point, what was done wrong. But this is not true in the area of writing.

What would happen if Green had asked the boss, "Just what am I doing wrong?" Most likely, Brown would have replied, "I'm not an English teacher! You went to school, didn't you? Just do it right!"

Why would he give such a brush-off answer? The truth of the matter is that most of the time the boss hasn't the foggiest notion of what Green has done wrong. All the boss knows is that he doesn't like it.

Some years ago, an article entitled "What Do You Mean I Can't Write?" appeared in *The Harvard Business Review* (May –June 1964).* This article, in terms of reprints, became a runaway best seller and ended up being labeled by the editors as an "all-time *Harvard Business Review* classic." One reason for this article's success was the fact that it contained a checklist itemizing the various mistakes a writer could make in a piece of business writing.

After the *Harvard Business Review* article and its checklist came out, we imagine the following scene took place in many of the nation's corporations. Green comes to the boss and says, "What don't you like about my writing?" Brown looks at his watch and says, "I'm busy now, Green. See you in half an hour." Brown then rushes to his office and locks himself in. But, instead of secretly revising the drafts before him, he now gets out the checklist and some copies of Green's correspondence. He proceeds to dope out just what it is about Green's writing that he doesn't like.

---

*Portions of this book reflect ideas developed in John S. Fielden's *Harvard Business Review* article "What Do You Mean I Can't Write?" (May–June 1964). Copyright © 1964 by the President and Fellows of Harvard College, all rights reserved.

Then, when he has the ideas written down, he calls Green in and is able to cite chapter and verse about what Green is doing wrong. The checklist gives businesspeople the critical vocabulary they need in order to evaluate written messages and to communicate their evaluation to others.

Therefore, we begin our book with a revised and expanded checklist even though many of the items in it may not be very meaningful to you until you have read the discussion that follows. But we must follow our own advice.

In this book we tell you to let your reader know *immediately* the purpose of your communication. So, dutifully, we tell you that this entire book shows you the dos and don'ts of effective business writing, as summarized in the checklist. Remember, the focus of the book is not only on how you personally can write better, it is also on how you can work with others and how you can be better able to discuss good business writing in commonly understood terms.

But, while working with others is valuable and necessary in modern offices, improvement begins with *you*, learning what good business writing is and then demanding it of yourself.

HOW TO USE THIS BOOK

After you have read this book, keep it on your desk. Reread parts of the book from time to time. Commit the checklist to memory. You will be sure to appear more knowledgeable than Brown when it's your turn to evaluate an important memo or report.

Each of us must be able to talk about writing with other people—without insecurity or embarrassment. It is foolhardy to regard managerial writing as something delicate, perhaps even sacred, that cannot be talked about frankly. Unfortunately, most businesspeople feel more comfortable talking about religion, politics, and sex than they do talking about writing.

Don't expect miracles from this book or yourself. Writing improvement comes from diligent practice over time. Unless you know what good, effective business writing is, you can't even begin to make progress. You can't reach a goal if you have no idea what that goal should be.

Our book is simple and it is clear. By striving to put its principles into your daily practice, we are sure you will become the efficient and effective writer you have always wanted to be.

LETTER-WRITING PERFORMANCE INVENTORY

1. MECHANICS

Grammar

Number Mistakes

_____ Faulty agreement between subject and verb.
_____ Faulty agreement between pronoun and noun it refers to.

Coherence Mistakes

_____ Dangling bricks.
_____ Misplaced bricks.
_____ Failure to develop a logical progression of ideas through coherent, logically organized paragraphs.

Vague Pronouns

_____ Pronouns with no clear referents.
_____ Pronouns with more than one possible referent.

Punctuation

_____ Misuse of commas.
_____ Misuse of *'s*.
_____ Unintentional fragmentary sentences.
_____ Creating run-together sentences by joining two sentences with a comma (instead of a semicolon or a comma plus *and, or, but,* or *nor*).

2. PROCESSING

_____ Typos and/or spelling mistakes.
_____ Improper format (e.g., use of internal memo format in external letters).
_____ Omissions, repetitions, and other evidence of careless proofreading.

3. READABILITY

Familiarity of Words

_____ Words not conversational.
_____ Inappropriate jargon or specialized shop-talk unfamiliar to the reader.
_____ Pretentious language (too much Latinate and too little Anglo-Saxon).
_____ Unnecessarily abstract or legalistic words.

Sentence Structure

_____ Sentences too long and rambling (too many compound sentences).

_____ Failure to blend complex and simple sentences for variety.

_____ Inappropriate use of passive voice.

_____ Failure to use normal sentence order (subject, verb, object) as much as possible.

Paragraphs

_____ Failure to use dashes, parentheses, or numbered or lettered lists to improve readability of lengthy series of thoughts in sentences.

_____ Paragraphs longer than three to four sentences.

_____ Failure to itemize and indent when needed to improve readability.

4. ADAPTATION AND ORGANIZATION

Adaptation

_____ Failure to tailor letters as much as possible to individual reader's educational level, position, personality, and the like.

_____ Failure to appear to focus on the *reader's* interests rather than those of the writer or the company (too many *we's* and *I's;* too few *you's).*

Organization

Ineffective Yes Letters

_____ Failure to give good news at the beginning.

_____ Failure to seize opportune time to ask for counter-favor from recipient of good news.

_____ Begrudging tone; failure to sound pleasant while doing what the reader wants.

Ineffective No Letters

_____ Failure to begin on pleasant or at least neutral tone.

_____ Failure to educate the reader, to give reasons for refusal, usually before giving the refusal.

_____ Giving appearance of expressing insincere sorrow when saying no.

_____ Failure to say no in terms of benefit to the reader, rather than to the writer or organization.

_____ Failure to let negative inference be drawn by reader, where possible and appropriate, instead of giving a blunt no.

_____ Failure to end letter with (1) an offer of a substitute for what was refused, or (2) a complete shift to something more pleasant.

_____ Seeming to pass the buck or blame somewhere else in the organization for the no decision.

_____ Offering a transparent alibi that insults the reader's intelligence.

Ineffective Persuasive Letters

_____ Failure to state request clearly and immediately.

_____ Failure to show why action desired by writer is to reader's interest.

_____ Failure to convince reader, by use of meaningful evidence, that action requested is reasonable.

_____ Failure to close by specifying how, when, and where desired action should be taken by reader.

_____ Failure to make desired action as simple as possible.

_____ Appearing too cagey, too transparently manipulative, where subtlety and finesse are called for.

5. THOUGHT CONTENT

Clarity and Completeness

_____ Verbose and rambling content, seemingly so pointless that the reader must ask what is desired.

_____ Purpose not thought through, so message does only half the job and necessitates further correspondence.

_____ Communication too brief; fails to incorporate obviously needed information; reader must write to ask for more.

_____ Failure to answer all questions asked by correspondent.

Analysis

_____ Superficial analysis of data.

_____ Conclusions unjustified by evidence presented.

_____ Seemingly extraneous data.

_____ Failure to qualify tenuous assertions.

_____ Failure to recognize and justify assumptions used.

_____ Exhibition of possible bias, conscious or unconscious, leading to distorted interpretation of data.

2

HOW TO TAKE THE GRR!
OUT OF GRAMMAR

People tend to refuse to admit their shortcomings and they tend even more to avoid doing anything about those shortcomings. Most people do know that they are woefully ignorant about grammar. But few, if any, ever take steps to overcome their ignorance.

That is why it is both dangerous and yet necessary for us to take up grammar here in section 2. It is dangerous because businesspeople typically hate and fear grammar—so much so that they may simply stop reading at this point. By discussing grammar so early in the book, we are, in effect, serving up a nourishing but bland vegetable first instead of a tasty literary bon-bon.

But it is necessary to serve grammar first because grammar—like wholesome food—is better for you than are humorous bon-bons. Furthermore, once you understand how logical and simple grammar is, you will lose your fear of it and take the necessary steps to acquire an understanding of why some writing is correct and some is not.

SO YOU THINK YOU KNOW EVERYTHING ABOUT GRAMMAR

We are concerned that some readers (liking to hide their ignorance) will complain that this book is too simplistic. In case you fall into this category, let us ask you to take a very simple pretest, just to see where you stand and whether what follows *is* beneath your level. (If it is, no harm done. Just skip ahead to section 3).

PRETEST

Identify the grammatical errors in the following ten examples Don't rewrite them; just name the error.

1 A few offices have consistently processed more than 40 percent of the month's activity in the last three work days. Attached for your information and appropriate action are a list of those offices that fall into this category.

2. An inventor may qualify for one or more award points for an Invention Plateau Award only if they are regular employees.

3. The capabilities and resources of each functional area is defined below.

4 After considering the current productivity requirements in the field, it is incumbent upon us to ensure that we spread the workload as evenly as possible across the entire month.

5. We have decided to hold a national managers' meeting June 4–7. We have also decided to continue holding regional meetings yearly. This should please most in-state managers.

6. Neither the warehouse in Cleveland nor the Dallas transportation department have responsibility for delivering equipment to the exhibit site.

7. Originally designed for use in the personal computing and research environment, the applications of ABCD have proved wider than planned.

8. After setting the headcount requirement, it will be necessary to move ahead to make our New York group responsible for developing an effective regional sales force.

9. The ability to develop hard-hitting A/V presentations and to deliver them effectively is the mark of a real professional. Customers expect these from top salespeople.

10. After analyzing the data, a decision was made to go ahead with production of the 6362 Model C 1 Printer attachment.

The correct answers to these examples are given at the back of the book.

Isn't it about time that you do something about making yourself comfortable with grammar? The first step is to admit your problem. Your problem is not real ignorance; you just have a mental block about grammar.

TWO QUESTIONS TO HELP YOU REMOVE YOUR MENTAL BLOCK

How many readers will admit they have a mental block? We think an extremely high percentage will. If you're a member of this vast majority, let's get to work on removing the block.

How would you react if we told you that if you can answer yes to just two simple questions, you already know 90 percent of all the grammar you need to know to be an effective business communicator? You'd probably say we were crazy.

Wait a minute before you reject our statement! Take a look at the two questions first. See if they don't seem as ridiculously easy as we claimed.

1. Do you believe that something (a word or an idea) *cannot* be singular and plural at the same time?

    Yes   No

2. Do you believe that words that relate to or influence the meaning of other words *should* be placed as close as possible to the word or words they influence?

    Yes   No

If you've answered yes to these two questions, we are pleased to tell you that you do indeed already know 90 percent of all the grammar you really need to know in order to be an effective business writer. You have stated that you can correctly identify two types of mistakes:

1. Number mistakes
2. Coherence mistakes

These two types of mistakes constitute the vast majority of grammatical mistakes made by businesspeople. And you, as the manager of your own and others' writing, should be able to identify these mistakes when they appear in letters or memos for which you are responsible. That is, you should be able to do this only if you trust your common sense about number and coherence mistakes. However, most businesspeople allow their foolish mental blocks to get in the way of their common sense.

OVERCOME THE ORIGIN OF YOUR MENTAL BLOCK

How did you acquire your mental block concerning grammar? Most of us got a start on it in our early school years when our English teachers presented us with 300-page books on grammar. We were forced to try to memorize the hundreds of rules in the book, rather than to recognize the logic behind grammar.

All that you gained from this experience was your mental block—a conviction that grammar was difficult, beyond your grasp. Much of it is, but, thankfully, most of the difficult aspects are so abstract that they are absolutely useless for people out in the trenches of the day-to-day business world. Only English teachers know (or claim to know) the 10 percent of grammar that falls into the difficult category.

Let's attack your mental block by facing three simple facts you may never have really thought about before:

1. Clear writing is clear thinking.
2. Words are the footprints left by your thoughts as they proceed across a page.
3. Grammar is the mortar that binds words (and ideas) together—the logic that enables a reader to understand the logical relationships among the words you have written.

If grammar is logical then we should be able to translate it into a series of principles that are sensible, obvious, and easy to remember. That's exactly what we are going to do throughout this chapter.

ATTACKING GRAMMAR
THROUGH TWO COMMON-SENSE PRINCIPLES

Let's take our two simple questions and turn them into the first logical principles we will use to rebuild your confidence about grammar.

PRINCIPLE 1. SOMETHING (A WORD OR AN IDEA) CANNOT BE SINGULAR AND PLURAL AT THE SAME TIME.

PRINCIPLE 2: IDEAS (OR WORDS) THAT RELATE TO OR INFLUENCE THE MEANING OF OTHER IDEAS (OR WORDS) SHOULD BE PLACED AS CLOSE AS POSSIBLE TO EACH OTHER IN A PIECE OF WRITING.

Both number and coherence mistakes are violations of these logical principles. Let's begin with number mistakes.

A. A number mistake is a violation of the first logical principle that something cannot be singular and plural at the same time.

B. There are two types of number mistakes:

1. Lack of number agreement between pronoun and antecedent.

2. Lack of number agreement between subject and verb.

We are going to assume that our readers know what subjects and verbs are. But we are not going to make the similar assumption that you know what the antecedent of a pronoun is.

First of all, a pronoun is nothing more than a word that takes the place of a noun. A noun, of course, is the name of a person, place, or thing. The antecedent of a pronoun is the noun that the pronoun replaces, the word that the pronoun stands for. It's the word the pronoun gets its meaning from. For example, the word *it* means nothing unless you know what *it* refers to— perhaps a contract. The word *she* means nothing unless you know who *she* is—maybe Mrs. Thurston.

HOW TO AVOID PRONOUN–ANTECEDENT MISTAKES

You probably have some recollection of your English teacher proclaiming, "A pronoun must agree with its antecedent in gender, number, and person." This statement illustrates one of the well-intentioned ways in which English teachers confuse youth. For all practical purposes this grammar-book statement is two-thirds useless. Let's prove it.

Consider gender. What native English speaker—even someone with little or no education—makes mistakes in pronoun gender? No one! One of the rare good things about the patched-together mother tongue of English is that (unlike most other languages) it uses logical gender. In English, the gender of a word is the same as the gender of the thing described. A girl is *she*. A boy is *he*. A desk is *it*. No one in any U.S. corporation is going to write, "The disk file capacity needs to be enlarged. Order her by Friday." Or, "Mary Smith asked me to contact you about the 3732 Secretarial Work Station. He thought you could give me specific information on its applications."

Also, don't worry about person mistakes. No one—regardless of his or her native tongue—mixes up first, second, and third person.

But do be concerned about number mistakes. Educated Americans at the higher levels of American industry are not willing to accept number mistakes in important business papers. This is not just because a grammatical mistake reflects badly on the writer's education, but also because of the legal problems that may result from faulty agreements of pronouns.

It's fine on the sports page to write, "Notre Dame is always a fine football team. They hope to win all their games next year." *Notre Dame* is singular. *They* is plural. We've already said that it's illogical and downright impossible for a thing to be singular and plural at the same time. But the nation's sportswriters regularly perform such grammatical miracles.

But what about an important business document? Consider the following:

> A committee of our financial executives is to meet with their counterparts from U.S. Amalgamated Industries to discuss the disagreement over financial terms. They are authorized to reduce terms by up to 10 percent.

Because of a shift in number, the reader is confused about who disagrees. The *committee* is singular. *Their counterparts* is plural. *They* is plural. Who are *they*? The committee or U.S. Amalgamated's executives? Grammatically, *they* would have to mean U.S. Amalgamated's executives, but we suspect the writer meant the committee. Documents dealing with business transactions—unlike the sports pages—have to be clear. And it is pretty difficult to be clear when you're contradicting yourself about singular and plural.

HOW TO AVOID SUBJECT–VERB NUMBER MISTAKES

Most of the subject and verb number mistakes we have found in business communications result more from carelessness in dictating or sloppiness in transcribing than from ignorance. You wouldn't write, "Smith and I is going to call on this customer." In the interest of keeping this book short, we're not going to belabor the obvious. Let us just comment on a few examples of slightly tricky subject–verb number disagreements worthy of your attention.

  1. The capabilities and resources of each functional area is defined below.

The writer here mistakenly assumes the phrase closest to the verb *(each functional area)* is the subject. It is not. The subject, *capabilities and resources* is plural and therefore demands the plural verb *are,* not the singular *is.* Remember that the subject of a sentence will not appear in a prepositional phrase.

  2. A few offices have consistently processed more than 40 percent of the month's activities in the last three work days. Attached for your information and appropriate action are a list of those offices that fall into this category.

Here the writer is confused about whether the subject is singular or plural. The word *are* indicates that the writer is thinking of either *your information and appropriate action* or *those offices.* Unfortunately, neither is the right subject. The subject is the attached *list,* which is singular.

  3. Neither Hertz nor National bill our company for drop-off charges on any one-way rental.

Here is a tricky one. When there are two subjects separated by *nor* or *or,* the verb must agree with the subject that follows the *nor* or the *or. National* follows *nor,* and *National* is singular, so the verb should be *bills,* not *bill.*

HOW TO CORRECT THE MOST SERIOUS WRITING PROBLEM IN BUSINESS: COHERENCE ERRORS

Coherence errors are violations of the second logical principle that ideas relating to or influencing the meaning of other ideas should be placed as close as possible to each other in a piece of writing. When business people don't follow this principle, they write incoherently. This is the most serious writing problem in business. All other problems are trivial by comparison.

There are two types of coherence errors:

1. Misplaced modifiers
2. Dangling modifers

Now, if you are like most people, the terms *misplaced modifier* and *dangling modifier* strike terror in your heart. Actually, the concept of correct modification is very simple. It all depends on how you look at it. We suggest you begin to think along the following lines.

REMEMBER BRICKS AND COMPILERS TO CORRECT COHERENCE MISTAKES

The only truly original writer is the poet. A poet puts novel ideas together; he or she puts words together in a way that they have never been put together before. The resulting word combinations are fresh, they are original, and they are just the opposite of clichés. But they are hard to read, they're different and unfamiliar, and they're compressed. In American business, happily, no one expects you to write poetry. All you are expected to be is a good bricklayer.

All of us have a storehouse in the back of our minds, a brickyard full of stock words and phrases. Sure, they're clichés; sure, they're unoriginal. But what difference does that make? Few people in business (except for creative writers in advertising) care about originality in writing.

All most managers care about is that you, as a writer, reach into your mental brickyard, select the bricks you need, and then put them on the page in a logical, coherent fashion. Here is brick

1—it goes first. Brick 2 goes next. Brick 3 follows brick 2. Then we see bricks 3a and 3b—obviously, they must go between bricks 3 and 4. Brick 5 concludes the sentence. (See figure 2–1) That's fine—you put your bricks on the page in that logical sequence. The reader's mind has no trouble following and understanding your thoughts and is quietly most appreciative.

FIGURE 2–1. Coherent sentences lead logically from one word (thought) to the next, like well-laid bricks.

Since *brick* is a word we are going to be using a lot, let's establish a quick definition. A brick is a unit of thought that must be positioned coherently among all of the other units of thought in a piece of writing. A brick can be a word, a phrase, a clause, a sentence, a paragraph, or even an entire section of a report. Words can be out of place logically, as can phrases, clauses, paragraphs, or report sections. When they are, we call them simply *misplaced bricks*.

In teaching businesspeople we have found it useless to stress the names of all of the types of words, phrases, and clauses that exist. (There are, for example, seven kinds of pronouns. Most businesspeople would be hard pressed to name just one type.) None of us remembers much, if anything, about these technical terms from any part of our formal education. In business, it's not important to know the names of the various kinds of bricks. But it is important to understand the crucial necessity of putting the units of thought (the bricks) together coherently. And, remember, by *bricks* we mean:

- Words within sentences
- Sentences within paragraphs
- Paragraphs within letters and reports
- Sections within reports
- Divisions within long reports

Good writers recognize this principle and strive to put their bricks together so that what they have written appears logical and understandable to the reader. In short, it's coherent.

But the bad writer takes his or her bricks, puts them into his or her mental wheelbarrow, and dumps them onto the page in a jumble. Then this writer says to the reader, "You sort them out! You figure out what I mean." That's what the writer has done in the following jumble of bricks masquerading as a memo. (See figure 2–2.)

FIGURE 2–2. Incoherent sentences are jumbles of words (thoughts), like piles of bricks.

TO: Branch Managers

FROM: Director of Management Training

SUBJECT: Management Effectiveness Conference

We have unless circumstances precluded scheduled the next Management Effectiveness Conference to be attended by all management personnel not otherwise burdened by administrative necessities for the night of January 11 and all day January 12; therefore you should expect to be advised provided you signify your intended participation before November 30 by Bill Swanson of hotel, dinner, and theater reservations for the first night of the Conference, January 11. The Management Effectiveness Conference is part of our managerial recognition program, the agenda of which is attached—meeting to be held in the Twelfth Floor Conference Room—and will be attended by an outstanding manager and GM from each Region/District. Giving people attending an overview of your area, wedding, where permissible, status report on current problems and the outlook for next year would be an excellent use of your time on the agenda. Coordinating the area if you have any questions is Jim Shapely.

The amazing fact is that we can indeed understand this terribly written, incoherent memo. We have become so used to bad prose that we have developed a sort of compiler in our minds. This compiler translates incoherent prose into some semblance of coherence and allows our brains to receive and process (i.e., understand) the information presented.

THREE LEVELS OF INCOHERENCE: HOW YOUR COMPILER RESPONDS TO EACH

The notion of the compiler is extremely important. We are going to ask you to bear it in mind because we will come back to the compiler again and again. But in order to understand how your compiler operates, you first need to recognize the levels of incoherence it has to attack.

Let's begin a process of self-discovery by looking at a sentence that shows the first level of incoherence:

Profits will never save the company, if kept at a minimum.

Remember, you agreed earlier that words or ideas (or bricks) that are related to or influence the meaning of other words (or bricks) should be placed as close as possible to each other in a piece of writing. You agreed because that is consistent with the way your brain is programmed. Look at our sample sentence and divide it into its component bricks:

Profits	will never save	the company,	if kept at a minimum.
(subject)	(verb)	(object)	(modifying phrase)

Note that the brick *if kept at a minimum* is placed next to the brick *company*. Therefore, the only way your brain can process that sentence logically as it is actually written is to view the *company* as that which is being kept at a minimum. But when you do, your brain immediately cries, "That doesn't make any sense!" So your brain turns on its compiler, which moves the brick *if kept at a minimum* over next to *profits* (where the *minimum* brick belongs). Now your brain can process the revised sentence ("Profits, if kept at a minimum, will never save the company.") because the sentence's words (or ideas) are now arranged coherently. All of this compiler activity happens unconsciously— and in microseconds.

Let's look at an example of the second level of incoherence:

I'm happy to sign your petition protesting pollution of our city's lake, which I am enclosing in this envelope.

If you were sitting in a training session instead of reading this book, you would join in the general laughter. Why would everybody laugh? The first thing our brains do, when we read something silly and incoherent, is to make us laugh. We do not know why this laughter occurs, but everybody recognizes that incoherence of this type is a source of much humor. (It was Groucho Marx's stock in trade. "I once shot an elephant in my pajamas," said Groucho. "How he got into my pajamas I'll never know!")

Now your brain, which tries its best to be logical, looks at the brick *which I am enclosing in this envelope* and notes that it is next to and apparently modifies *lake*. Naturally, your logical brain thinks this juxtaposition of ideas is ridiculous and laughable. Your brain simply cannot process illogical, incoherently presented data. As a result, the brain's compiler has to cut in and ask, "What *is* it that is being enclosed in the envelope?" The *petition*, of course, is the answer—not the lake! So the compiler rewrites this sentence as follows:

> I am happy to sign your petition protesting pollution of our city's lake. The signed petition is enclosed.

In the world—but not in the world of business, we should surely hope—there is an even more difficult level of coherence. Suppose you come across a sentence like this one:

> Very important to consider, the least important consideration deciding on an impulse.

What can your compiler do with this? It cuts in and tries to make sense out of the sentence by moving the bricks around. But there is no sense to be made. The bricks are absolute gibberish and completely preclude mental editing. The compiler, in effect, gives a nervous giggle and considers pushing the laughter button.

There is something about words without sensible meaning that frightens our logical brains. Perhaps you have known an aged person who, having suffered a stroke, is unable to talk coherently. The result is pitiful and terrifying. This level of incoherence, of course, seldom concerns us in our day-to-day business communications. We just want you to be aware of how readers react to various types of incoherence. The mildest reaction they will exhibit from first-level incoherence will be fleeting irritation. The second level will cause them to laugh at you. Neither reaction is desirable.

HOW YOUR COMPILER WORKS

Let's focus on level one and analyze how your compiler works and what causes irritation. Recall our guinea pig sentence:

Profits will never save the company, if kept at a minimum.

An occasional sentence like this, awkward and incoherent though it may be, really causes the readers a minimum or discomfort. The compiler cuts in and—whisk!—the bricks are rearranged in a coherent fashion so that the brain can process the information rapidly. This all happens so quickly that the readers are not even conscious of it. But consider our example of second-level incoherence:

I am happy to sign your petition protesting pollution of our city's lake, which I am enclosing in this envelope.

Here there is no possibility that the readers won't realize that their compilers have to go to work. The compiler laughs, and the readers think the writer is a fool.

But you need to know more about how the compiler works. The compiler is like a dash runner, not a long-distance runner. It can operate only for short periods of time without apparent psychological discomfort. If you ask typical readers (like yourself, for instance) to read a memo like the one on the Management Effectiveness Conference, they will experience a hair-pulling sensation of "This is awful! This is terrible writing! Reading this is like trying to stick your head through a stone wall!"

Why does the reader's compiler register such psychological discomfort when a letter like this has to be read? Suppose we were to ask you to rewrite the Management Effectiveness Conference memo. How long would it take you to really rewrite it so that it is completely coherent?

We think that even the best of editors would take some time just to figure out what the writer is talking about. The editor then might spend fifteen to thirty minutes rewriting the memo in a perfectly coherent fashion. But how long did it take you to read the original and to battle your way through to some semblance of understanding? Just a matter of a very few minutes. Consider that.

Do you really appreciate what a fantastic mental exercise your brain just performed? It edited—in a matter of minutes—a piece of incoherent writing and made it coherent and understandable. And it did all this in midair, so to speak, without pencil and without paper. This was a phenomenal and exhausting mental exercise. The psychological energy required leaves the brain depleted. Can you imagine how exhausting it would be to force your compiler to wade through a ten-page report written by such a writer? Bad writers put their readers through this task every time they try to communicate.

Let's summarize what goes on in messages written by and for company personnel. There is the writer of the message, the sender. There is the reader, whose mind is relentlessly logical and can process bricks of information only if they are presented in a logical fashion. And in the reader's mind there is a compiler that cuts in to edit (mentally) badly written stuff, to arrange the bricks so that the brain can process (understand) the ideas contained in those bricks (units of thought).

Remember, writers have compilers, too. And their compilers are naturally biased in favor of whatever the writer has writtten. Suppose you are evaluating the coherence of a letter a colleague has written. You point out the incoherencies to that colleague. But the truth of your analysis probably will not be immediately obvious to the writer. Individuals' compilers are a function of their own brains and, hence, they know full well what the writers meant to say even though the words didn't actually come out right.

Many people we have counseled can look at a sentence they have written, as obviously incoherent as "Profits will never save the company, if kept at a minimum," and not be able to recognize the essential incoherence. So, when you counsel others about writing, be aware that *you* will be able to identify their mistakes a lot more readily than *they* will.

And when you edit your own prose, recognize that you must turn off your own compiler so that you can examine your own sentence bricks with ruthless detachment. Don't worry if you find that you have not written with perfect coherence. Few of us can do so in a first draft. Just take that draft, turn off your compiler, find the misplaced bricks, rearrange them coherently, and you will have a communication that clearly and logically expresses your thoughts. Your readers will not have to call upon their compilers to edit mentally what you have written.You will have done it for them. That's what good writers do.

HOW THE COMPILER WILL HELP YOU MANAGE WRITING AND WRITE MORE EFFECTIVELY

In order to teach others and learn for yourself how to write effectively, you have to understand in detail how the compiler works. We will oversimplify so as to make the compiler's function crystal clear. Let's begin by looking at a very simple sentence.

A set of activities will be initiated for each product leading to an Assessment Report.

This sentence can be read easily enough, but only after your compiler has rearranged the bricks. Consciously, you are not aware of your compiler's activity. But, if you reduce the sentence into component units of thought, you will see that you cannot process the bricks as written:

1	2
A set of activities	will be initiated
3	4
for each product	leading to an Assessment Report.

Obviously, brick 4 does not modify or relate to brick 3. How does your compiler proceed? Let's picture the compiler as a sort of derrick with a hook hanging from its boom. When the compiler wants to move a brick, it lowers the boom, puts the offending brick on the hook, and tries moving the brick to different locations.

In this case, your brain has difficulty processing the brick *leading to an Assessment Report* because that brick does not modify *for each product*. The compiler asks, "What *does* it relate to? What will lead to an Assessment Report?" Obviously, brick 1, *a set of activities,* is the answer. So the compiler moves brick 4 next to brick 1.

The compiler quickly sees that in this situation it can sensibly drop brick 4 in back of or in front of brick 1. The main difference is whether the writer wants to emphasize *leading to an Assessment Report:*

4	1
Leading to an Assessment Report,	a set of activities
2	**3**
will be initiated	for each product.

or *a set of activities:*

1	4
A set of activities	leading to an Assessment Report
2	**3**
will be initiated	for each product.

But, in some instances, a brick's capacity to modify forward as well as backward can have a devastating effect. Suppose, for example, you decided to add a fifth brick to the sentence, a brick that read *in order for us to get a better understanding of the field environment.* The sentence now reads:

1	2
A set of activities	leading to an Assessment Report
3	**4**
will be initiated	for each product
5	
in order for us to get a better understanding of the field environment.	

Immediately, the reader's compiler cuts in and discovers that brick 5 modifies brick 1. But look what would happen if you put brick 5 in back of instead of in front of brick 1:

A set of activities in order for us to get a better understanding of the field environment leading to an Assessment Report will be initiated for each product.

You see here that the compiler can test only by context which brick position makes sense. If you leave the example as it is

(1–5–2–3–4), the compiler has to determine—by context—that brick 5 modifies brick 1, not brick 2. The trick in sharp, coherent writing is to arrange bricks of thought so accurately that the reader's compiler does not have to cut in. The thoughtful writer would therefore arrange the bricks so that the reader knows that brick 5 modifies only brick 1, as follows:

> In order for us to get a better understanding of the field environment, a set of activities leading to an Assessment Report will be initiated for each product.

HOW TO CORRECT MISPLACED MODIFIERS

Now that you understand the principle of the compiler, let's take a look at misplaced modifiers. The concept of a misplaced modifier is quite simple. Let's examine some examples.

1. The Industry Newsletter contained an explanation which was detailed and penetrating of implementation plans by the coordinator.

Note how your compiler operates. Your brain finds it impossible to process the brick *implementation plans* when it is followed with *by the coordinator.* It asks, *"What is by the coordinator?"* The answer is *an explanation by the coordinator.* Your compiler has just corrected a misplaced modifier.

2. Our Canadian division has provided us with the current requirements under the Canadian Immigration Act for temporary entry into Canada, which is attached.

The final brick—*which is attached*—can modify either *current requirements* or *for temporary entry,* or even *Canada.* Your compiler has to cut in and figure out which modification is more logical. Obviously, the brick in question modifies *current requirements.* But why should a sloppy writer force the reader to figure out what in the world the writer means? The correct way for an intelligent writer to compose this sentence, your compiler tells you, is: "Our Canadian division has provided us with the attached current requirements under the Canadian Immigration Act for temporary entry into Canada."

Now let's look at two of our pretest sentences.

3. After considering the current productivity requirements in the field, it is incumbent upon us to ensure that we spread the workload as evenly as possible across the entire month.

This is an interesting example of how your compiler works unconsciously. If you turn off your compiler and force yourself to read what the writer actually wrote (not the instant revision your compiler presents to your brain), you'll see that *it* is what is *considering the current environment.* Remember, earlier you said that your brain was programmed to believe that words that relate to each other should be placed as close as possible in a piece of writing. Well, isn't *it* as close as possible to the *considering* brick?

What's happened, of course, is that your compiler—as quick as a flash and completely without your conscious knowledge—has rewritten the sentence to put the word that is doing the considering where it belongs, that is, next to the phrase that begins with the word *considering.* What your compiler presents to your conscious brain is: "After considering the current environment, we decided to spread the workload." Wouldn't it be nice if writers wrote accurately the first time so that we wouldn't have to use our compilers, consciously or unconsciously?

4. Originally designed for use in the personal computing and research environment, the applications of ABCD have proved wider than planned.

Here's the type of incorrect statement your compiler handles so easily that you are not even aware that anything has been mentally edited. But, if you assume—rightly, we think—that the brain cannot process illogically presented data, the compiler has to operate. *Applications* is the closest noun to *originally designed ....*" But how can *applications* be originally designed to be used? It's nonsense! There's a brick out of place. What was *designed for use* in the sentence? *ABCD*, of course, not *applications.* Hence, this is what your compiler actually presented to your brain for processing:

ABCD, which was originally designed for use in the personal computing and research environment, has proved to have wider applications than planned.

Some readers will note that there are many ways the sentence could have been rewritten. That, of course, is true. Since sentence structure is discussed later in the book, let us say only that any proper revision should begin with the brick that is *really* the subject being talked about. If the writer's real subject is *applications,* the sentence should be rewritten like this:

> The applications of ABCD, which was originally designed for use in the personal computing and research environment, have proved to be wider than planned.

HOW TO CORRECT DANGLING MODIFIERS

What happens if your compiler discovers that there simply isn't any word in a sentence that is modified by the brick dangling from its hook? What can your compiler do when there is no logical place to drop the brick in question?

The answer is *nothing.* The brick continues to dangle on the hook; hence, the famous and once-terrifying term *dangling modifier.* Now that you understand the principle of the compiler, the term *dangling modifier* actually makes literal sense. A dangling modifier is nothing more than a brick left dangling on the compiler's hook! Consider this example:

> After deciding on a course of action, the best strategy seemed to be to buy, not make, the components.

After you divide the sentence into bricks, your compiler asks, "Who is deciding on a course of action?" The compiler then finds itself facing the choices illustrated in figure 2–3.

Which brick is *deciding on a course of action*? The compiler draws a blank. The brick modifies nothing! More accurately, it modifies something the writer has not put into the sentence. Dangling modifiers are actually modifying what we call the secret subjects. The writer does have a subject in mind, but he or she has neglected to put that subject into the written sentence. Therefore, the reader can only guess who is doing the deciding.

If someone you work with wrote this sentence, you could give instructions for the subject to be put back into the sentence. The result might be this:

> After deciding on a course of action, management believed that the best strategy seemed to be to buy, not make, the components.

But when a letter or memo is written to someone hundreds of miles away, the reader can only guess who the secret subject is. Then, the dangling modifier becomes an extremely dangerous

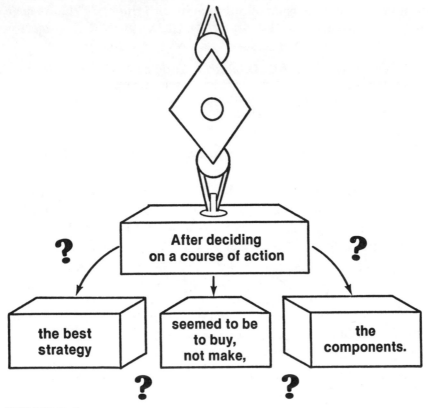

FIGURE 2–3.

type of mistake for managers to make. It allows the reader's compiler to invert the subject you failed to include. And readers may very well invent a subject that suits *their* convenience, not yours.

Let's look at a few instances in which a dangling modifier allows readers to do just that.

1. After setting the terms for payment for tapes and disks, it will be necessary to take up the matter of quality assurance.

Who is setting the terms for payment? Your company? The customer's company? What will readers quickly assume?

2. Using the given figures, my department clearly bears no responsibility for the contractual failure.

Who is using the given figures? Who is deciding that the writer's department bears no responsibility? Certainly, *my office* can't use figures. There's no word in the sentence that can use figures. Here's a case where a clever writer is using the secret subject to imply that *anyone* using the given figures would exonerate his or her office from blame.

HOW TO AVOID DANGLERS

Most religions exhort their followers to avoid the occasion—or opportunity—for sinning. In other words, if you're on a diet, stay out of the candy store. Are there ways to avoid dangling modifiers? Dangling modifiers have a penchant for following introductory bricks that begin with participles. That's fine, you say, but what's a participle? A participle is nothing more than an action word ending in *ing*—for example, *ordering, opening, operating, analyzing, deciding.**

Why do introductory bricks beginning with participles cause trouble? Take a look at the following brick:

Programming the computer, ...

What does your mind tell you should follow the brick? Your mind is programmed to believe that the next subject is going to be the person or thing doing the action described by the participle, that is, *programming the computer*. Note that we said next *subject,* not the next *noun.* In the example, the next noun is *computer,* that which is being programmed, not the person who is doing the programming. The person who is doing the programming must follow as the subject of the sentence. If not, you have a secret subject and a dangling brick.

Consider another example:

Running the Retirement Benefit Plan, ...

Who is running the plan? Your mind is programmed to believe that the next subject is going to be the person running the plan.

In case there is any doubt about the way your mind is programmed, here are a couple of comical examples:

After swimming three laps in the pool, drinks were served.

---

*There is another kind of word ending in *ing*—a gerund. A gerund is a participle used as a noun: "Swimming is fun." Don't worry about gerunds; they can't dangle.

Did you laugh? Did your compiler push the laughter button at the thought of drinks swimming three laps in the pool?

Walking down the street, the stone lion in front of the library came into view.

Did you think it ridiculous to imagine a stone lion walking down the street?

You laugh because your mind is programmed to believe that the first subject following a participle brick is the thing that is doing the action expressed by the participle. Now let's turn to some business examples:

Analyzing in detail the individual answers collected and comparing them with the plenary group positions, information about the effectiveness of this learning experience can be obtained.

Ask yourself, "Who is analyzing and comparing?" Certainly not *information*. A secret subject is doing the analysis and comparison. The only way to correct this sentence is to rewrite it to include as its subject the person or persons doing the analysis and comparison. Something like this will do:

The researchers, analyzing in detail the individual answers collected and comparing them with the plenary group positions, obtained information about the effectiveness of this learning exercise.

Here's another example:

Knowing Fortran, Helen's computer experience qualified her for the job.

Who knows Fortran? Certainly not Helen's computer experience! True, *Helen* is in the sentence, but she is not the subject. She's there only as an adjective, modifying *computer experience* (telling whose computer experience it was). But it is not the computer experience that knows Fortran. Since there is no subject in the sentence that can know Fortran, the brick *knowing Fortran* dangles.

BE SUSPICIOUS OF SECRET SUBJECTS

Once you are aware of the notion of the secret subject, you can keep people from ducking responsibility for actions they report. Suppose you were the boss and the following sentence was in a report from a subordinate:

After analyzing the data, a decision was made to recommend importing, not locally manufacturing.

Immediately upon spotting the participle *analyzing,* you ask, "Who analyzed the data? Who made this recommendation?" You request a revision. When the sentence is next presented to you, it reads:

After analyzing the data, George Jones and I decided to recommend ...

Based on experience, we conclude that dangling bricks and resultant secret subjects occur most frequently by far when people are reporting something bad, something negative, or a situation in which they (or others they are shielding) have made an embarrassing mistake. Secret subjects also occur most frequently, as one might expect, in reports going *up* in the organization. If experienced managers spot a sentence like this being reported up in the organization, they become immediately suspicious:

Basing projections on estimated declines in market, it was recommended that production be severely curtailed.

Veteran secret-subject-spotters could almost bet that the market did *not* decline and that production should *not* have been curtailed. The person responsible has grammatically gone underground to hide.

HOW TO AVOID BEING VAGUE WITH YOUR PRONOUNS

Many communication problems in business result from vague pronoun usage. Undoubtedly, that's why lawyers long ago coined such phrases as *party of the first part, party of the second part,* and *hereafter referred to as....*
One maxim that all readers need to remember is this:

> PRINCIPLE 3: NEVER TRUST A PRONOUN. AVOID USING PRONOUNS AS MUCH AS POSSIBLE. CHECK THOSE YOU MUST USE FOR NUMBER AND COHERENCE.

Just look at the beginning of this memo:

In a recent difference with BETA and CER Corporations, the country offices had responsibility for transmitting to the customers all relevant costs to be expected in installing the 3730 Distributed Office Support System. They had no authority to the contrary, and they should have understood that incidental costs would be charged to them. They were instead vague.

They certainly were vague. But who are *they*? *They* cannot refer to both the customers and the country offices. Readers, not knowing which company *they* is, freely substitute whatever meaning suits their convenience. Lawsuits frequently result from such vague pronoun references.

But you can't get through life without using pronouns, so you might as well understand something about pronouns and how your brain is programmed to use them.

Earlier in this book we said that if you could answer yes to two questions, you already knew 90 percent of what you needed to know about grammar. Happily, pronoun clarity falls into that 90 percent category. Vague pronoun reference is simply another violation of principle 2 (ideas relating to or influencing the meaning of each other should be placed as close as possible to each other.)

In fact, a pronoun has no meaning until the reader infers that meaning from the pronoun's location relative to the nouns in the sentence. Thus, coherence in the use and placement of pronouns becomes doubly important.

> PRINCIPLE 4: AN ENGLISH READER'S BRAIN IS PROGRAMMED TO BELIEVE THAT THE NOUN NEAREST A PRONOUN AND AGREEING WITH IT IN GENDER AND NUMBER IS THE ANTECEDENT OF THAT PRONOUN.

Here's a comical example, just to convince you of the truth of principle 4:

If raw milk does not agree with the baby, boil it.

Why did you laugh? Your brain is programmed to believe that the nearest noun agreeing with *it* in gender and number is what is being boiled—*the baby!* After you stop laughing, your compiler cuts in and rearranges the bricks so that the sentence makes sense.

They finished their assignments but they were too late.

The second *they* can refer to either *assignments* or the first *they*.

You are programmed to believe the reference is to *assignments,* but you are not sure. Your compiler is helpless when faced with such a vague pronoun. If you *had* to make a choice, the compiler would go along with its usual programming and assume that the assignments were too late, because *assignments* is the nearest plural, neuter noun to *they.*

> All sophisticated corporations should insure themselves against disaster and the consequent loss of vital records. It provides for the resumption of corporate activity in as short a period of time as possible.

Your compiler can't handle this one. What does *it* refer to? The nearest singular, neuter noun is *loss;* next is *disaster.* In a sense, this sentence contains a dangling pronoun, because there is no noun in the sentence (as written) that can be the antecedent of *it.* We guess that *it* refers to the act of insuring the corporation, a brick that is not in the sentence.

> The manager told the director he was wrong.

Again, the compiler is perplexed. According to the rule, *he* should refer to *director.* But does it? Only the vague writer knows!

> Arrange either desks or chairs for seating so that they will be able to take notes if they so desire.

What does *they* refer to? *Desks* or *chairs,* the nearest nouns? Your compiler wonders, "Can desks and chairs take notes?" Of course not! But who are *they?* This is a vague, even dangling, pronoun.

> Sales and production have agreed on the use of a new technique, which should please Mr. Brown.

Here's a good example. What should please Mr. Brown? The new technique? Or that the sales manager and production have agreed on something? As written, that *which should please Mr. Brown* refers to *technique,* the closest singular, neuter noun.

> He offered to resign, but it was refused.

This is a classic example of how your compiler quickly will invent a reference for a pronoun that a poor writer leaves dangling. The *it* here does not refer to any noun in the sentence (*offered to resign* is a phrase, not a noun). The compiler performs its usual magic and turns *offered to resign* into *offered his resignation,* creating a noun. Your mind thus is able to process the following, which the writer meant to write:

> He offered his resignation, but it was refused.

Here is one last example:

> Supermarket Communication Systems are dramatically changing data management for supermarket chains. It allows chains with between four and twenty stores to transmit and receive data on price changes, sales, check verification, and checker performance."

The trouble here is with *it*. The nearest neuter, singular noun is *data management*. But how can data management receive and transmit data on price changes, sales, check verification, and checker performance? The writer has fallen into a typical pronoun trap. If the writer hadn't waved his or her arms, so to speak, and had used nouns instead of a vague pronoun, the sentence would have read, "Such systems allow chains with ..."

> ---
> PRINCIPLE 5: BECAUSE A PRONOUN MEANS NOTHING UNTIL A READER KNOWS WHAT NOUN IT REFERS TO, ALWAYS PUT THE NOUN FIRST AND THEN FOLLOW WITH THE PRONOUN.
> ---

Let's look at an example:

> Perhaps it was not made clear, but it had been discussed over several months; so surely all managers have had a chance to discuss this change in policy.

Until the reader gets to the end of the sentence, he or she does not know what *it* refers to. Wouldn't the sentence have been far clearer (and more easily readable) if it had been written this way?

> Perhaps this change of policy was not made clear, but it had been discussed over several months; so surely all managers have had a chance to discuss it.

A poor writer really causes vague pronoun trouble when he or she writes a puzzler like this:

> Perhaps it was not made clear, but the criteria have been defined in several ways.

Here the compiler really gets thrown a curve ball. *It* is singular. *Criteria* is plural. Does *it* refer to *criteria*? Has the writer simply made a number mistake? Or does *it* dangle, referring to a noun not in the sentence? Applying our maxim—begin with the noun and follow with the pronoun—would help (even though the sentence is, of course, still wrong):

> Perhaps the criteria was not made clear, but it was defined in several ways.

It is fairly clear now that we are dealing with a number mistake. The writer, having never heard of the word *criterion,* thinks *criteria* is singular. Your compiler fixes the mistake quickly.

3

HIGH- AND LOW-IMPACT WRITING

To be an effective business writer, you need to know how to make your written communications achieve the effect you intend and desire.

When businesspeople write something, they usually want someone at the other end to be able to read it. Moreover, they usually want that person to be able to read it with ease and immediate understanding. (We say *usually* because there are times, of course, when people write things that they really *don't* want people to understand.)

When you are writing material that you want people to be able to read easily, you need to create high-impact writing. When you are writing material that you don't want people to read easily, you create low-impact writing.

High-impact writing and low-impact writing involve different ways of using sentences, words, and paragraphs:

- High-impact sentences are easy to read and to understand; low-impact sentences are boring and difficult to understand.
- High-impact words are familiar and easy to interpret; low-impact words are strange and difficult to interpret.

- High-impact paragraphs contain thoughts that leap off the page into the reader's mind; low-impact paragraphs contain hidden thoughts and are displeasing even to look at.

We will begin our discussion of high- and low-impact writing with the sentence, go on to word choice, and end with the paragraph.

HOW READERS' MINDS RECEIVE INFORMATION

PRINCIPLE 6: READERS' MINDS ARE PROGRAMMED TO RECEIVE LANGUAGE INFORMATION IN A SUBJECT–VERB–OBJECT ORDER. PUT THE SUBJECT FIRST, AS MUCH AS POSSIBLE, FOR HIGH-IMPACT SENTENCES.

Most of you will read this principle and say, "So what?" Actually, there is no more important point to be made in this entire book than the fact that the English-speaking mind receives information in a way that is symbolized by the subject –verb–object order of a sentence. The mind asks about *any* message, "What is the subject? What are you talking about?" Next, "What actions are being taken by the subject?" And, finally, "What is the object or effect of these actions?" This principle is the building block on which you can base much of your understanding of how to communicate with people in English.

In order to prove this point, we ask you to look at a few examples. As you read these examples, ask yourself what is actually happening in your mind.

1. Of assistance in designing a system tailored to a customer's needs is....
2. As I consider the titles of the different discussions to be held, especially those of Mr. Valento, the subject matter to which I am to address myself, and the divergent interest of the group....

What has happened in your mind? Are you comfortable as you read? Is what you read being processed in your mind? Or, rather, is your mind attempting to store this information until something happens, until your brain learns something? What *is* that something that the mind is waiting for? It is waiting for the subject, of course.

WHY YOU NEED A SUBJECT

To see this need for a subject, read the other half of these two sentences:

1. The attached checklist will be ...
2. My concern is that my remarks may not be on target ...

What happens in your mind here? Your mind is processing the information as fast as you read it, because your mind has been given a subject. Now look at the two sentences in their complete forms:

1. Of assistance in designing a system tailored to a customer's needs is the attached checklist.
2. As I consider the titles of the different discussions to be held, especially those of Mr. Valento, the subject matter to which I am to address myself, and the divergent interest of the group, my concern is that my remarks may not be on target.

Both sentences are inverted or written backwards. The subject is withheld until the latter part of each sentence. This impairs understanding.

There are, in effect, three funnels by which information reaches the language-processing part of our minds: a subject funnel, a verb funnel, and an object funnel. Under the subject funnel is an ignition switch.

When the subject goes through the subject funnel, the subject supplies the key to ignite the mental language-processing machinery. (See figure 3–1.)

If no subject is sent through the subject funnel to key the switch, words sent through the verb and object funnels merely stack up. No processing of data occurs. Your mind is busy, desperately trying to store the information until it is told the subject.

Imagine that you are in your office one day and a fellow worker pops in and says, "Reason 1, reason 2, and reason 3, reason 4, and reason 5, reason 6," and so on, to reason 15. Desperate, you hold up your hand. "Stop!" you cry. "Reasons for what?" "Reasons why Bill Smith is not the right person for that

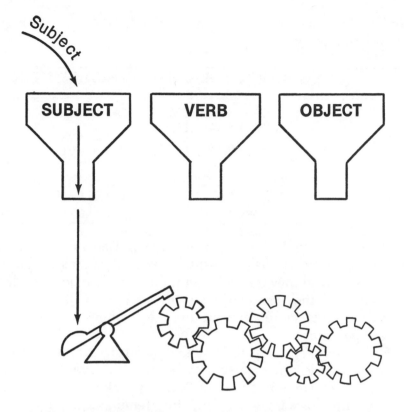

**Subject passing through subject funnel trips switch,
turning on the brain's language-processing machinery.**

FIGURE 3–1. Processing of a normal subject–verb–object sentence.

job!" she answers. "Oh!" you say. "What were those reasons
again?"

Your mind is being asked to store up fifteen reasons when
your brain doesn't even know what the subject is. The fact that
you say "Oh! What were those reasons again?" shows that
nobody's mind can be asked to store up a whole bunch of objects
of some unknown subject. People need to know what the subject
is.

That is why we say that principle 6 is so basic to effective,
high-impact communication. It doesn't matter whether you are
talking about a sentence, a paragraph, a memorandum, a
report, or an entire book. It doesn't matter whether the communication is spoken or written. The receiver needs to know
what the subject is before any kind of data can be processed.

Giving the reader the subject immediately is the key to high-impact communication.

HOW TO WRITE HIGH-IMPACT SENTENCES

> PRINCIPLE 7: FOR SENTENCES WITH HIGH IMPACT AND HIGH READABILITY:
>
> 1. USE SIMPLE SENTENCES AS MUCH AS POSSIBLE.
> 2. TRY TO AVOID COMPOUND SENTENCES.
> 3. BE SELECTIVE IN YOUR USE OF COMPLEX SENTENCES.

Most people in the business world are harried and busy. Most deeply resent having to sift through *any* kind of prose, high- or low-impact. And they certainly put no premium on longwindedness. In this, they are markedly different from their teacher friends who seem to dote on prolixity, long sentences, and longer paragraphs.

Furthermore, if the practical-minded future executives chose to use a simple sentence style of writing in school, they frequently were chided for being "choppy." The argument that since choppiness was good enough for Hemingway it ought to be good enough for the teacher fell too often on deaf ears. To future businesspeople, it seemed as if complex stylists such as Faulkner and Joyce were prized too highly and that simplicity in prose was too much ignored.

Scolded for overusing simple sentences, future businesspeople were forced to glue their simple sentences together with connecting words such as *and, but, or,* and *nor.* As a result, all they did was to make long, boring compound sentences out of short, clear, high-impact simple sentences.* Compare these two versions of the same memo:

All of you have been kept aware of the studies conducted by Corporate Personnel Research in 198– and 198–. Many of you and your staff members assisted with them.

The Management Effectiveness Studies were presented to the president on March 28, 198–. The attached letter contains a summary of the conclusions and actions being taken.

---

*For those of you who would enjoy a refresher about what constitutes a simple, compound, or complex sentence, turn to the appendix on punctuation.

The seventh point in the summary states that appropriate guidelines are being developed to improve the management identification and selection process.

These identification and selection guidelines will be provided to the operating units in the third quarter of this year. We should avoid attempting to establish a universal set of specific management selection criteria.

All of you have been kept aware of the studies conducted by Corporate Personnel Research in 198– and 198–, and many of you and your staff members assisted with them.

The Management Effectiveness Studies were presented to the president on March 28, 198–, and the attached letter contains a summary of the conclusions and actions being taken.

The seventh point in the summary states that appropriate guidelines are being developed to improve the management identification and selection process, and these identification and selection guidelines will be provided to the operating units in the third quarter of this year, but we should avoid attempting to establish a universal set of specific management selection criteria.

Don't you agree that changing the sentences in this memo from simple to compound lowers readability? Then why do people continue to use compound sentences in so much of what they write? Probably it's because they have difficulty unlearning those admonitions against choppiness.

To prevent students from giving their readers a break by bisecting compound sentences, the instructors told them, "Thou shalt never begin a sentence with *and, but, or,* or *nor.*" There is no such rule in the real world. Look at the productions of the world's finest writers to find that such a prohibition never disturbed them. Let us proclaim a different rule: "You can begin a sentence with anything you like as long as the sentence begins with a capital letter."*

Complex sentences don't seem to bother readers because there is usually a close, logical relationship between ideas in both

------

*You must begin a sentence with a capital. It is unacceptable in many areas of writing for you to write a sentence like this: "13 is an unlucky number." You have to write, "Thirteen is an unlucky number." We don't challenge this rule because it makes sense in technical writing. If a sentence began with *13* the reader might be confused (in technical or scientific prose) and believe that the period that ended the sentence before actually went with the *13* that began the next sentence. Therefore, it is argued that careless readers (or careless typesetters) might read, ".13 is an unlucky number."

clauses. The reader's mind is led along smoothly right to the end of the sentence. We doubt if you'll have any difficulty in reading these complex sentences:

1. Corporate will not approve implementation of mortgage interest and area rate differentials because both are very expensive and, once introduced, difficult to discontinue.
2. Although several operating units indicated an interest in the proposal, the degree of participation varied greatly.
3. Because these responses have been received and the changing needs of the operating units have been made clear, we feel it is not appropriate to pursue the concept of corporate coordinated staffing centers under national contracts at this time.

Let us summarize our suggestions about high-impact and low-impact sentence structure:

Don't worry about choppiness when you are writing a routine meat-and-potatoes type of business communication.

There is nothing wrong with writing, "The detailed improvements to the International Assignment Plan are attached. These improvements will become effective on July 14. Please disseminate these changes as appropriate." We have never met a business person who was upset about receiving a memo that contained a series of short, choppy, simple sentences. All businesspeople want to know is the facts, as quickly as possible. So why not give them exactly that?

When you are writing something that requires a little style and variety, merely add some complex sentences to the mix of simple sentences.

These will remove the possibly choppy appearance of your writing without doing any particular damage to readability. (Remember, now that you are permitted to start sentences with *and, but, or,* or *nor,* there is no longer any need to write compound sentences.)

A GUIDE TO DETERMINING WHEN TO USE THE PASSIVE VOICE

Almost every book about writing has warned writers to avoid the passive voice. This is all very well except that most readers of these books have little understanding of what the passive voice really is. And those few who do know what the passive voice is really have little understanding of just *why* the passive voice causes trouble for the reader.

In order to explain the trouble, let us ask you first to recall the concept of the three funnels channeling words into your brains. Let's use these funnels to illustrate the difference between a passive and an active sentence and why one is so easy to understand and the other is so difficult. (See figure 3–2.) Here is an active, simple sentence:

Mr. Donnelly reviewed the operating plan.

Mr. Donnelly is the subject. *Reviewed* is the verb. *Operating plan* is the object. Each of these thoughts drops neatly through the subject, verb, and object funnels, and the sentence is processed.

Now let's look at the same sentence expressed passively:

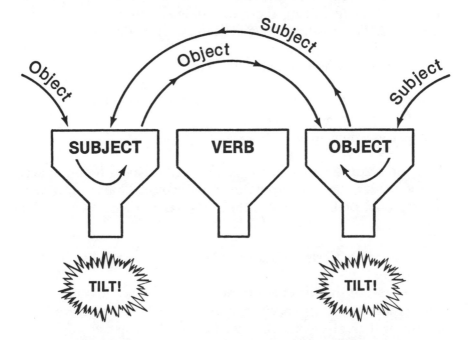

Compiler must reject the object from the subject funnel and reject the subject from the object funnel in order to start the brain's language-processing machinery.

FIGURE 3–2. Delayed Processing of Passive Voice Sentence.

The operating plan was reviewed by Mr. Donnelly.

Now what takes place in your brain? Isn't there a momentary delay? That is caused by the need for your compiler to cut in. The writer has played a trick on your brain. He or she has tried to put the object, *the operating plan,* down your subject funnel, and he or she has tried to put the subject, *Mr. Donnelly,* down the object funnel.

Your brain cries, "Tilt! Something's wrong!" Your compiler cuts in, kicks the object out of the subject funnel, throws the subject out of the object funnel, and reinserts them down the correct funnels. The compiler then processes the sentence as it should have been written: "Mr. Donnelly reviewed the operating plan."

As you have seen repeatedly, every time you force readers' compilers to cut in, you are causing psychological discomfort. You are making it more difficult for readers to read what you've written. You are forcing them to edit mentally what you have presented. That is why writing teachers warn people to avoid the passive voice.

In summary, then, the passive voice:

1. Forces the reader's compiler to rewrite sentences mentally.
2. Lowers and softens impact.
3. Makes writing dull.

If you are trying to write prose that will register a high-impact on the reader, stay away from the passive voice. That is why most writing books tell you to avoid the passive.

HOW THE PASSIVE VOICE CAN BE YOUR FRIEND

But most of the writers of these books have not had much, if any, experience in the business world out where there are real people with real emotions; where a poorly constructed letter doesn't get a failing grade, it loses a customer, a job, the respect of subordinates, or the approval of superiors. And in this real world, a wise use of the passive is often called for.

So let's talk realistically about the passive voice in the context of high-impact and low-impact writing. When *should* the passive voice be used?

PRINCIPLE 8: THE PASSIVE VOICE DRASTICALLY LOWERS
IMPACT. USE PASSIVE VOICE ONLY WHEN:

1. FOR DIPLOMATIC REASONS YOU WANT
   TO HIDE THE SUBJECT FROM THE
   READER.
2. YOU DO NOT WANT NEGATIVE IDEAS TO
   LEAP OFF THE PAGE.

Look at the most elemental of situations where someone might want to hide. This situation can be symbolized by one simple sentence:

I made a mistake.

Assume that this sentence and others like it appear in a report you have to write to an important customer to say that a mistake you've made is going to cost the customer money. The sentence, "I made a mistake," becomes the cause célèbre of the entire report. Somehow, as you look at the sentence, it seems to focus unwanted attention on you. Let's see how the passive voice can be useful in such an embarrassing situation; let's change "I made a mistake" to the passive. Now the statement reads like this:

A mistake was made by me

That is a bit of an improvement. At least the *I* is not up there, front and center, as the one who made the mistake. You've been relegated to the back of the line, so to speak. Nevertheless, you are still in the line and are not happy about that. Once more the passive voice can ride to the rescue with a simple adjustment: Now the sentence reads:

A mistake was made.

Where did *you* go? Who made the mistake? What happened to you? Who is the customer going to be mad at? In your heart you know that if there ever was a time for a secret subject, this is it!

Now let's take this simple example and expand it, still using the same psychological principles. Compare two contrasting memos dealing with typical situations.

Suppose you are Director of Personnel. You recently discovered that a young assistant of yours, Bill Haddenfield, has been suggesting to other personnel managers that they should consider using company stock as an award for special recognition programs. You like Haddenfield; he's a good assistant, but he should have checked with you before spreading the idea around. Furthermore, for a number of reasons (the stock is not available in some countries, and there are legal ramifications in others) these stock awards cannot be used.

When you call Haddenfield in to gently reprimand him and explain why this idea cannot be implemented, you learn that he has spread the idea far beyond the scope that you can handle through personal meetings. You have to write a memo to all personnel managers to clarify the policy on giving out company stock as an award. Suppose you dictate and send out the following memo:

TO: Personnel Managers

FROM: Director of Personnel

One of my assistants, Bill Haddenfield, has suggested to many of you that you consider using company stock as the award for special recognition programs in countries where stock purchase is available.

Bill failed to check with me before making this suggestion and did not realize all the implications of this kind of award.

Please remember that under no circumstances should you use our stock as an award, whether purchased by an individual or the corporation. A variety of U.S. Securities and Exchange Commission regulations preclude such gifts for award transactions. And we wish to avoid confrontations with these rules.

This is good high-impact writing, full of punch, direct, and clear. What do you think Haddenfield will do? How will he feel about this memo? What effect will this memo have on his morale? How will others who deal with Haddenfield feel about him? Perhaps the situation could have been handled as effectively and clearly but more tactfully if the passive voice had been used. If you were Haddenfield, would you feel as hurt by this memo?

TO: Personnel Managers

FROM: Director of Personnel

Recently a suggestion was made to use company stock as the award for special recognition programs.

Under no circumstances should our stock be used in this manner, whether purchased by an individual or the corporation. Such gifts are precluded by a variety of Securities and Exchange Commission regulations, and confrontations with these rules are to be avoided.

While the passive voice is useful in situations like the one described above, it can be used as a means of hiding important information from readers in authority over the writer. Whether this is good or bad depends on whether you are the hid*er* or the hid*ee*. Let's compare two contrasting memos dealing with an imaginary but tough situation and see which approach you prefer.

Let's say that three months ago your team held up introduction of a hot new product. You held up the product based on the recommendation of your immediate superior. Later events proved this decision to be a serious mistake. Headquarters asked for an explanation of the mistake and an analysis of its possible ramifications. Which of these two versions would you prefer to sign?

Version I

TO: Pat Jones, President

FROM: Kim Johnson

Bill Jones, my product manager, made the primary mistake. He was careless in his analysis of market data. He should have spotted the discrepancy between sales forecasts and economic forecasts. His mistake will cost the company:

1. Our main customers
2. Our profit for the quarter
3. Any chance to catch up with our competition

cc Bill Jones

Version II

TO: Pat Jones, President

FROM: Kim Johnson

It could be concluded that an unfortunate mistake occurred as a result of inadequate analysis of data. Apparent discrepancies between sales and economic forecasts should have been detected. Lost will be some primary customers as well as profits for the quarter. It is also possible that chances to catch competition will be minimized.

Version I is obviously high-risk, especially since Bill Jones is your boss. Unless you are ready to put everything on the line in an attempt to capture his job, you might want to give serious consideration to signing version II. Here, the use of the passive voice masks the identity of just who is responsible. Things just happened. No one was responsible. Which of the two versions do you think Bill Jones would prefer?

It is not our purpose to advise you to be evasive. It is our job to show you how to be evasive if, in a given situation, you want to be. All we are saying is that if you are ever forced to respond in writing to a sensitive issue, and you really do not want to be specific and open, then consider using the passive voice. It will help you to hide. And because passive writing is backwards, it is slow and boring to read.

But, in judging other people's writing, you must be appropriately suspicious if subordinates' reports are couched in passive terms. Since the passive voice is another way of masking the secret subject, the passive will be used largely in negative situations. If you are the boss, make subordinates use the active voice so that responsibility can be pinpointed.

HOW TO CONTROL WORD CHOICE

Our advice on choosing words for high-impact business writing can be summed up in two simple principles:

> PRINCIPLE 9: READERS DON'T LIKE (OR UNDERSTAND) MANY LATINATE WORDS; HOOKING LATINATE WORDS TOGETHER CREATES GOBBLEDYGOOK.
>
> PRINCIPLE 10: READERS DO LIKE (AND UNDERSTAND) MOST WORDS FROM THE ANGLO-SAXON. MOST CONVERSATION USES WORDS DERIVED FROM ANGLO-SAXON.

What most people refer to as "big words," "ten-dollar words," or "gobbledygook" are, 99 times out of 100, words that have entered English from the Latin by way of Norman French.

When most people in U.S. corporations write, "Terminate the illumination," instead of, "Shut off the light," they are reacting to a phenomenon that began one afternoon in A.D.1066. On that day at the Battle of Hastings, William the Conqueror downed King Harold and his Anglo-Saxons and created our strange, schizophrenic modern English that has at least two words for almost everything. One set of words comes from Teutonic ancestors, the Anglo-Saxons. The other set comes from Norman ancestors, whose Norman French descended from popular Latin. Ever since that time, these two types of words have battled for supremacy in English usage.

Socially, undoubtedly because the French won in 1066, the deck has been stacked in favor of Latinate words. English teachers, lawyers, medical practitioners, government bureaucrats, military personnel, academicians, and even the menu writers in American restaurants, all favor Latinate words.*

As a matter of fact, isn't inflated language one of the general public's greatest annoyances? People have even gone to court to force gobbledygook out of contracts, insurance policies, health plans, and the like. The general public understands and trusts Anglo-Saxon words far better than it does Latinate words.

Let's not belabor this point. We understand that many of you will find it hard to agree that it is not only all right but desirable to use familiar words in writing. Nevertheless, it's a principle of high-impact writing.

PRINCIPLE 11: IF YOU WRITE AS YOU SPEAK, AND USE THE SAME ANGLO-SAXON WORDS, READERS WILL UNDERSTAND YOU BETTER.

Common, ordinary, Anglo-Saxon words convey sincerity. Was it an accident that Lincoln's Gettysburg Address contains very few Latinate words? That the translators of the King James version of the Bible used almost no Latinate words? That Winston Churchill didn't say, "Sanguinity, perspiration, and lachrymosity"? If Anglo-Saxon words were good enough for these great communicators, they ought to be good enough for you.

---

*In our pastures and pens, we see cows, pigs, and sheep—good old Anglo-Saxon animals. But what happens when these animals appear on the menu? *Voila!* They become high-class. They change into words from the French: beef (*boeuf*), pork (*porc*), and mutton (*mouton*), Only a foolhardy menu composer would write "Roast Pork Butt," in words drawn from Anglo-Saxon instead of the French.

HOW TO ENGINEER PARAGRAPH IMPACT

Whether or not you want what you write to be highly readable is up to you. If high impact is desired, observe the rules of principle 12. If you want low-impact, do just the reverse.

PRINCIPLE 12: FOR HIGH-IMPACT PARAGRAPHING:

1. USE SHORT PARAGRAPHS. PEOPLE FIND THEM MORE READABLE THAN LONG ONES.
2. ITEMIZE AND INDENT MULTIPLE IDEAS IN PARAGRAPHS.
3. ALLOW PLENTY OF WHITE SPACE ON THE PAGE. READERS UNCONSCIOUSLY REACT FAVORABLY TO IT.

If your subject is highly favorable and agreeable to readers, you want your ideas to leap into their minds, not just lie there on the page. Use short paragraphs and lots of indented lists, and let plenty of white space hit the reader's eyes.

If your topic is negative and disagreeable to readers, then your ideas should not leap off the page to punch readers in the eye. Use long paragraphs, no itemized lists, and little white space.

If you are trying to sell the readers something or persuade them to do what you want, the ideas that benefit the readers should be highlighted, itemized, underlined, and surrounded by eye-catching white space. The cost to the reader (unless it is a great bargain) should be buried in a paragraph near the end of the letter.

In a nutshell, that's about all the strategy there is to paragraphing. Let's look at how we can make a few sample paragraphs more readable and higher in impact on the reader.

I. Low Impact

During the changeover from contract guards to security officers, the quality of the existing contract security service must be upgraded through the careful selection of vendors and implementation of acceptable contractual performance requirements. In those instances where guard services are provided by the landlord as part of the lease, appropriate negotiations must be conducted by Purchasing to terminate this service within the specified changeover time period.

(This paragraph scores low on readability because it's one big glob. That's fine if it's what you want. But if you want your reader to grasp your meaning quickly, write this paragraph as follows.)

I. High Impact

During the changeover from contract guards to security officers, the quality of the existing contract security service must be upgraded through:

1. The careful selection of vendors.
2. The implementation of acceptable contractual performance requirements.

In those instances where guard services are provided by the landlord as part of the lease, appropriate negotiations must be conducted by Purchasing to terminate this service within the specified changeover time period.

II. Low Impact

To qualify for the achievement award, a sales representative must accomplish one of the following. He or she must sign twenty new accounts, accumulate 10,000 sales points, or sell 100 installed units within one year.

II. High Impact

To qualify for the achievement award, a sales representative must accomplish one of the following within one year:

1. Sign twenty new accounts.
2. Accumulate 10,000 sales points.
3. Sell 100 installed units.

III. Low Impact

The key point is that all too few companies possess a fully integrated scheme for breaking down corporate objectives into man-size chunks; establishing individual performance standards; establishing wage, salary, and employee benefit structures; appraising performance at regular intervals; and rewarding or taking remedial steps on the basis of active performance.

III. High Impact

The key point is that all too few companies possess a fully integrated scheme for:

1. Breaking down corporate objectives into man-size chunks.
2. Establishing individual performance standards.
3. Gaining acceptance of performance standards.
4. Establishing wage, salary, and employee benefits packages.
5. Appraising performance at regular intervals.
6. Rewarding or taking remedial steps on the basis of actual performance.

IV. Low Impact

The customer utilizing repair center maintenance is responsible for determining when remedial maintenance is required, for removing and replacing machines in the operational environment, for checking machine performance while machines are installed in the operational environment, and for shipping machines prepaid to the repair center and utilizing designated containers available from the company for such shipment.

IV. High Impact

The customer utilizing repair center maintenance is responsible for:

1. Determining when remedial maintenance is required.
2. Removing and replacing machines in the operational environment.
3. Checking machine performance while machines are installed in the operational environment.
4. Shipping machines prepaid to the repair center and utilizing designated containers available from the company for such shipment.

4

ORGANIZING
FOR DESIRED IMPACT

When it comes to organizing thoughts in a letter or memo, there is one glaring error that nearly all businesspeople make: they usually have no idea of what they are going to say until they've said it.

For example, if there is a question about whether a customer's request is going to be allowed or rejected, most writers will respond by first running through all the arguments for and against the request. Then, at the end of the memo, they will announce their verdict.

All analytical letters of this type follow the same organizational pattern, whether or not the verdict is favorable to the reader's interest. This is wrong.

Here is the principle to keep in mind:

> PRINCIPLE 13: DETERMINE WHETHER YOUR COMMUNI-
> CATION IS POSITIVE OR NEGATIVE TO THE
> READER'S INTERESTS BEFORE YOU
> WRITE. IF IT IS NEGATIVE, ORGANIZE
> YOUR THOUGHTS ACCORDING TO THE
> NO-LETTER FORMULA. IF IT IS POSITIVE,
> ORGANIZE ACCORDING TO THE YES-LET-
> TER FORMULA.

USING THE NEGATIVE LETTER STRATEGY

It's amazing that all of the businesspeople we have counseled have known intuitively how to organize a negative communication. But while they may have known how, they usually did just the opposite when they actually wrote. See how you react to this case:

> You have a subordinate who is, at this point, too good to fire and too weak to promote. Today you're meeting with him to discuss his performance. You are not going to promote him, but you want to motivate him to improve in several areas as soon as possible. How would you structure your conversation in a face-to-face meeting?

In classes, people invariably choreograph the sequence of events as follows:

1. You make the subordinate feel comfortable with some shop-talk or extraneous small-talk.
2. You bring up the real topic of the meeting.
3. You know that you should not tell him no immediately. You do not want to make him feel rejected and defensive before the discussion of why has taken place.
4. You know that a full discussion of the reasons is important. The first thing that even your children say after you've told them no is "why?" You realize that adults react in the same way. Therefore, you want to educate your subordinate by offering the reasons for the no before you actually say no.
5. To make him feel respected, you acknowledge that he does some things well (say, A, B, and C).
6. But there are other things (D, E, F, G, H, I, J, K, and L) that he doesn't do well. He needs to show quick improvement.
7. To turn the conversation to a hopeful note (and into face-saving direction for the rejected subordinate) you state that if he can show improvement on some of D, E, F, G, H, I, J, K, or L, you will reconsider him for promotion in six months. You promise him full backing in this attempt to improve. (Naturally, if he is so dense as to ask, "Do you mean the answer is no?" you will tell him that he has firmly seized the obvious.)
8. You close on a business-as-usual note at the end of the interview.

This is exactly how a no-letter should be organized. People seem to use this organizational pattern in handling face-to-face negative situations. But they seldom write with the same kind of sensitivity to the reader's feeling that they reveal when there is a real human being at the other end of the communication.

Consequently, as soon as you determine that your message will be perceived as negative by the reader, organize your thoughts just as you would if you were talking to the reader face to face.

PRINCIPLE 14: ORGANIZE A NO-LETTER ACCORDING TO THIS FORMULA:

1. BEGIN ON A NEUTRAL NOTE. DON'T GIVE FALSE HOPE OR MISLEAD THE READER. BUT DON'T THROW A HARPOON IN THE FIRST PARAGRAPH.
2. INTRODUCE THE TOPIC.
3. EDUCATE THE READER. EXPLAIN WHY. GIVE THE REASONS UNDERLYING THE NEGATIVE DECISION THAT FOLLOWS.
4. EITHER SAY NO OR OFFER A SUBSTITUTE FOR NO (SUCH AS, "IF YOU IMPROVE IN SIX MONTHS, WE'LL RECONSIDER").
5. END ON SOME PLEASANT OR BUSINESS AS USUAL NOTE.

Notice how the following letter adheres to principle 14, as a corporate president rejects a suggestion made by one of her company's employees.

Dear Frances:

Thank you for your February 28 submission to our "If I were President of ABCD" program. Your recommendations relative to improving the Planning function were very much appreciated. Planning *is* an increasingly important area, not only in the division but throughout the corporation. Your ideas for improving the process are very good, and I want to comment on the specifics:

Centralized Planning Staff

As for your first suggestion, let me concede that this function is indeed understaffed. However, a plan has already been established to increase the department headcount.

The second part of your suggestion included merging several departments: Market Research, Forecasting, Corporate Planning, and Planning Control.

As you know, all but Planning Control are currently part of the same organization. Within this organization, Market Research and Forecasting are part of the same department. Planning Control has not been included because we feel it should not be an integral part of a department whose major responsibilities deal with the mechanics of producing the plan.

Planning Control was originally conceived as a management system whose primary mission was to control changes to the established plan, and this has been extremely effective. There have been several recommendations that Planning Control should be expanded to include the development of plans. We are currently investigating not only the question of expanding its function, but also its reporting structure under a new mission.

Management Plans and Practices

Your recommendation is sound. But the approach to planning that you recommend has previously been implemented.

For the reasons outlined above, your two specific recommendations will not be implemented, and this letter will also conclude their consideration under the "If I were President of ABCD" program. Nevertheless, I commend the thoughtful manner in which your ideas were presented, and I do appreciate your having brought them to my attention.

Sincerely,

To accomplish the steps outlined in principle 14—and, hence, to meet the reader's needs—a no-letter must be fairly long, as this example has shown. A brief no-letter is likely to be regarded by most readers as curt, brusque, insensitive, a slap in the face, or a brush-off. If you doubt this, consider what Frances's reaction would have been if she had received this letter instead of the one above:

Dear Frances,

Both of the suggestions you submitted to the "If I were President of ABCD" program have been rejected and will not be implemented. Better luck next time!

People like longer rejection letters, and not merely for the reasons suggested in principle 14. A long letter makes it appear as if the person doing the rejecting at least had the courtesy to explain the reasons fully. The writer regarded the reader and his or her request seriously. The writer did not simply give a blanket refusal without any consideration of the legitimacy of the case being considered. Longer rejection letters offer strokes that the readers of disappointing news often appreciate.

Take another situation. An inventor offered a patented idea to a large corporation for consideration and possible manufacture. Several months went by before the inventor learned that the corporation had no interest in his patent.

The inventor wrote an angry response to the management, belaboring it for taking so long a time just to say no. What kind of response would best soothe the angry inventor's feelings? Look at the following letter, which adheres carefully to principle 14:

Dear Mr. Smith:

Thank you for your letter of January 5 concerning the delay in advising you that we already knew about the basic ideas presented in your suggestion. I appreciate your candid expression of dissatisfaction, and, because you took the time to write, I believe that you are giving me the opportunity to clarify the conditions that caused delay.

The review of ideas and inventions received from outside the company is one of the areas we have not been able to automate. Every submission must be handled on an individual basis and reviewed by the appropriate people, who may be scattered throughout the organization. These engineers and marketing representatives, of course, have other prime duties, are often away on field trips of several weeks duration, and cannot always immediately respond to my request for an evaluation of a submitted idea.

I first sent your proposal to marketing requirements people in New York. They advised me that they are already aware of the basic idea, but because of work being done in our Georgia laboratory, they suggested that I forward your material there for consideration with the hope that there was something in your material that could be applied to a potential project under consideration. Our people agreed that your idea has potential but again found nothing in your proposal of which they were not already aware.

I am sorry about the delay and can understand your concern. However, in cases like this, when one group within the company suggests that another consider the material, I always feel that it is best to take a little more time and be sure that we have considered every aspect of a proposal before concluding that we have no interest in it. I assure you that the delay was caused only by our desire not to overlook anything that could be mutually beneficial.

Very truly yours,

This is longwinded, but it is probably true that you can't be too longwinded when saying no, at least from the rejected reader's point of view. How do you think the reader would react to this succinct response?

Dear Mr. Smith,

Regardless of the amount of time it took us to conclude that we had no interest in your idea, the fact remains that we don't.

Very truly yours,

USING THE POSITIVE LETTER STRATEGY

Yes-letters are easy. You can write, "Yes, you get the promotion," on a paper towel and hand it to a subordinate, and you will never get an objection. Does the subordinate demand a reason why? No. This is hardly true about negative messages. Tell a child, "No, you can't go out," and see if he or she doesn't say, "Why, Daddy?" or "Why, Mommy?" But say, "Yes, you can go," and the child is off like a shot, without a care about the reasons.

In other words, for the most part, don't worry about explaining all of the reasons why you are saying yes. Just say yes and quit.

> PRINCIPLE 15: ORGANIZE A YES-LETTER ACCORDING TO THIS FORMULA:
>
> 1. SAY YES IMMEDIATELY.
> 2. IF YOU HAVE ANY COUNTERFAVORS TO ASK WHILE THE READER IS EUPHORIC, ASK THEM. (BUT DON'T LOOK TRICKY OR BEGRUDGING!)

Sounds simple, doesn't it? Surely everybody would organize in this way. But most writers don't. We ask groups which of the following scenarios they like best. Imagine that you have bought a very expensive cashmere sweater but you don't like it. You want to return the sweater to the exclusive clothing store where you bought it.

Scenario I

You walk into the store and say you want to return the sweater. The manager says, "Have you worn it? Have you washed it? Has it been dry-cleaned? What's wrong with it? Why don't you like it? Is this a spot I see? Oh, by the way, our store always stands behind its merchandise. You can either get your money back or make an exchange."

Scenario II

You walk into the store and say you want to return the sweater. The manager says, "Our store always stands behind its merchandise. You can either get your money back or make an exchange. By the way, I need to ask some questions for our buyer's benefit. Have you worn it? Have you washed it?...."

Invariably, everybody votes strongly in favor of scenario II. Yet, when we give people a case involving a similar business situation, they organize their letters according to scenario I. The reason was mentioned earlier. They have no idea, when they start to write, whether or not they are going to give the customer his or her money back. They analyze the situation and arrive at the end of the letter at a conclusion favorable to the reader. So, by writing a history of how they thought, they inadvertently organize their yes-letter exactly like a no-letter.

This is just what happened to the writer of the following letter. The manager of a large business office wrote a strong complaint letter to the manufacturer of an automatic coffee maker. The manager claimed that the coffee maker used in her office apparently short-circuited and severely charred the top of the office table upon which it rested. Here is a disguised version of the letter that was sent in response:

Dear Ms. Payton,

Thank you for informing us of your regrettable experience involving a Jiffy Coffee Maker.

We are sincerely sorry to hear that a Jiffy appliance failed in the manner you described. We are aware, as we know you are, that a failure such as this is not a very pleasant experience. We wish to reassure you that failures such as you have reported are extremely rare because of the extensive tests and checks we make on our electrical devices. We have the best possible quality control procedures and are justifiably proud of the excellent quality of our products.

However, because you have been inconvenienced, we are sending you, under separate cover, a new Jiffy Coffee Maker, which we believe will give you satisfactory service.

We will reimburse you, within reason, for the cost of repairing your office table. Send us a copy of the estimate and, if it is fair, we will send you a check as soon as possible.

We appreciate your thoughtfulness in bringing the matter to our attention, and we hope your confidence in Jiffy will be restored.

The organizational pattern used in this letter dissipates very effectively most of the favorable impact that an early yes will have on the reader. How much more effective would this letter have been if it had followed the organizational formula recommended for good news messages in principle 15? See for yourself:

Dear Ms. Payton,

A new Jiffy Coffee Maker is being sent to you, with our apologies. Also, we would like to reimburse you, within reason, for the cost of repairing the damaged section of your office table. Send us a copy of the repair estimate and, if it is fair, we will send you a check as soon as possible.

Needless to say, we are sincerely sorry to hear that one of our coffee makers failed in the manner you described. We assure you that failures such as you have reported are extremely rare because of the extensive testing and checking we do on our electrical devices. We have the best possible quality control procedures and are justifiably proud of the excellent quality of our products.

Thank you for your thoughtfulness in bringing this matter to our attention. We hope your confidence in Jiffy will be restored.

USING THE PERSUASIVE LETTER STRATEGY

Honesty is the best policy, goes the old saying. And in writing persuasive messages in American corporations, honesty is probably the only policy.

It may be marginally acceptable for a direct-mail outfit to hoodwink the consumer with a devilishly persuasive (if misleading) letter. But in a corporation—or in written dealings between corporations—you had better not mislead, misrepresent, or seduce.

You have to live with the people you work with. They are not like some mail-order customer you can "sell" and forget. In the long run, the most effective way of being persuasive is to have earned a reputation for honesty and sincerity. Therefore, our persuasive letter formula differs in two important ways from the "sell-the-sizzle" type of formula found in many books on persuasive writing.

First, we advise you to be direct in your organizational pattern, unless the subject matter makes it absolutely necessary to be indirect. Don't try to hide the fact that you are asking something of the readers. Be direct and forthright, not cute.

Second, we caution against reading some text on direct-mail selling and applying that advice to a corporate setting. If you do, you may sound like a huckster.

PRINCIPLE 16: ORGANIZE A PERSUASIVE LETTER AC-
CORDING TO THIS FORMULA:

1. DON'T TRY TO CON YOUR READER. STATE YOUR REQUEST CLEARLY AND IMMEDIATELY.

2. SHOW WHY THE ACTION DESIRED IS IN THE READER'S OR THE COMPANY'S BEST INTEREST. BUT DON'T SOUND LIKE A HUCKSTER.

3. CONVINCE THE READER (BY USE OF MEANINGFUL AND HONEST EVIDENCE) THAT WHAT YOU WANT IS REASONABLE.

4. TAKE THE ORDER—SPECIFY HOW, WHEN, AND WHERE THE DESIRED AC-TION SHOULD BE TAKEN.

5. MAKE THE ACTION REQUIRED AS SIM-PLE AS POSSIBLE. ("JUST INITIAL A COPY OF THIS LETTER, SEND IT BACK TO ME, AND I'LL PLACE THE ORDER.")

Businesspeople are busy. Everybody is after them—not just you—wanting them to do what somebody or other wants. Therefore, you do have to get the reader's attention. You do have to explain clearly just what it is you want. And you do have to make it easy for the reader to do what you want. In these senses, a persuasive letter in a corporation does follow direct-mail persuasive techniques. But because you have forthrightly told your reader what you want in the first paragraph, you will not look manipulative.

You also don't want to adopt a writing style that makes you sound like you're giving a sales pitch. Look at this example:

TO: Branch Manager

FROM: Subordinate

How would you like to double the speed at which paperwork gets processed in this office? Wouldn't you be thrilled to learn that it is now possible to acknowledge orders far more promptly, straighten out complaints before they fester because of delay, and in general facilitate our ability to communicate better?

Such will be the case if you supplement the branch's word processing center with individual work stations for personnel in key positions.

Here are the details supporting this recommendation ...

There's nothing really wrong with the style of writing in this memo. But it jars; it seems inappropriate to the close interactive relationship between people in an organization.

What would this memo look like if it had adhered to the precepts of principle 16?

TO: Branch Manager

FROM: Subordinate

Based on considerable research, I recommend that you consider supplementing our word processing center with individual work stations for personnel in key positions. My analysis indicates that if you accept this recommendation, the following benefits may result:

1. The speed at which paperwork is processed will quite probably double.
2. The current backlog in acknowledgment of orders will be largely eliminated.
3. Delays in prompt dealing with customer complaints may well be a thing of the past.

Here are the details supporting this recommendation ...

USING THE INFORMATION LETTER STRATEGY

Letters that simply convey factual information should be easy to write. This would be true, of course, if:

1. People weren't so busy, and
2. Business types liked to read other people's messages and were willing to put aside their busy interests to focus on the writer's interests.

All of us are busy. And we are not usually sitting around dying to read what someone else has written. So smart writers frequently organize an information letter with as much care as they would a persuasive letter. They get the readers' attention right off by proving that the information being conveyed is important to the readers. If the writers can't make a case for its importance, they should admit this immediately.

Let us share an instance where such an admission would have proved helpful. An administrative assistant to the president had the task of coordinating responses to confidential complaint letters sent in by employees. This program was called "Plain Talk," and people writing in were guaranteed anonymity and freedom from reprisal. One Plain Talk was so sensitive that the assistant was asked to meet with the complainant immediately. The assistant subsequently wrote the following memo to the president:

> I met with the writer of the attached Plain Talk yesterday. We discussed the three factors on which his irritation was based ...
>
> (Paragraph 2 dealt with factor 1 at length. Paragraph 3 dealt with factor 2 at length. Paragraph 4 completed the process.)
>
> (Paragraph 5 ended the memo by stating:) The complainant has agreed that all issues have been handled satisfactorily. There is no further action expected of you.

How would you react, as president, to reading a five-paragraph memo only to discover that one paragraph—the last—was all you needed to read? It would have been far wiser if the assistant had written:

The Plain Talk issue you inquired about is resolved. The writer of the attached Plain Talk has agreed that all issues have been handled satisfactorily. There is no further action expected of you.

Attached is a summary of our discussion for your consideration, if you care to know more.

This revision arrives at the key point immediately, and the writer establishes quickly and simply the importance of the message by inserting the phrase *you inquired about.* This phrase not only reminds the president of the topic, but it also persuades him or her that it is a topic of some importance—after all, the president raised the issue.

Here's another example of imparting the attractiveness of a persuasive letter to a straight informational communication. Notice how the writer draws the reader in by dangling the carrots of improved response time, minimized problems, and ensured ease of growth.

December 15, 198–

A. D. Blue
Data Processing Manager
A & B Corporation
Government Product Division

Dear Mr. Blue:

Your staff and I recently conducted a preliminary study of the A & B system to determine what could be done to improve response time and minimize problems. We also looked for ways to ensure ease of growth and prevent future problems. Three areas that A & B needs to study in more detail became readily apparent to each of our team members:

1. Programming standards
2. Performance monitoring
3. Terminal operators training

Let me describe in some detail what we found in each of the above areas ...

PRINCIPLE 17: ORGANIZE AN INFORMATION LETTER AC-
CORDING TO THIS FORMULA:

1. FRANKLY TELL YOUR PURPOSE IN
WRITING AND WHY THE INFORMATION
CONVEYED IS IMPORTANT, UNLESS, OF
COURSE, THE REASON IS OBVIOUS,
SUCH AS WHEN YOU ARE ANSWERING
A QUESTION.

2. TELL THE READER WHY HE OR SHE IS BEING GIVEN THE INFORMATION. IS THERE ANYTHING THE READER IS SUP-POSED TO DO WITH IT?
3. IN OTHER WORDS, QUICKLY PERSUADE YOUR BUSY READER THAT YOUR MES-SAGE IS WORTH READING.

Failure to follow principle 17 usually results in make-work memos or mystery messages. And such uninformative letters are unfortunately omnipresent in business.

When we first started working with top executives in various companies, we asked them, "What bothers you most about bad writing in your company?" The answer was startling.

Almost to a person, these top managers answered, "Letters or memos that I don't know what to do with, or what is expected of me, or even why the writers have sent them to me. Letters like that end up causing *me* to have to write more letters saying, essentially, 'If you'd only tell me what your last letter said and what you want me to do, I'd be happy to consider it!'"

Here's a real example of this problem—synopsized, of course:

1. The top manager receives a letter from a subordinate. It says, "Jinny Gray is going to be in San Francisco next month. Please give me instructions."
2. The manager is nonplused and is forced to write back, "Why did you tell me that Gray is going to be in San Francisco next month?"
3. The reply comes promptly: "Because I thought you wanted to know!"
4. The manager: "I see no need for that information."
5. The subordinate: "Oh! Sorry."

Five letters concerning a fact, but a fact that means nothing out of context. The foolish subordinate (who just earned a black mark) assumed that the manager knew the context of the situation, but the manager did not. Why assume? Why not recognize that your memo amounts—in the life of a busy manager—to little more than if you popped into the manager's office, shouted, "Jinny Gray's going to be in San Francisco next month," and then bolted out the door again. "Huh? What?" says the boss, staring at the door.

How much better to clue the boss in on what you're really attempting to communicate:

About a year ago when we lost the XYZ account you said we should let the smoke clear and then try to get XYZ back as a customer.

Jinny Gray's going to be in San Francisco next month, and I thought this might be a great opportunity for us to pay a visit on XYZ. Jinny's always gotten along well with XYZ's top management. How about asking her to do a little missionary work? I think it's time. Do you? If it's okay, just initial a copy and send it back to me. Thanks.

5

PUTTING IT ALL TOGETHER: A PRACTICAL LANGUAGE FOR WRITING IN BUSINESS

Throughout this text we have discussed a number of different skills—mechanics, word choice, sentence structure, and organization, to name a few. And you may be tempted to conclude that writers who have mastered these areas must naturally be labeled good writers by their readers. Unfortunately, this assumption is not valid. It is certainly true that mastery of these skills increases the likelihood of successful communication, but it does not ensure it.

People who write successfully in the difficult world of business know full well that the communication process does not consist simply of writers putting their words down on paper. They never forget that on the other end of their messages are people—people with varying emotional makeups and needs, people with more or less power over us and our job futures.

Perhaps some of you remember a puzzle that is often posed in high school physics classes. The physics teacher asks, "If sound is defined as the physiological result occuring when sound waves strike the ear drum of a listener, then does a tree falling in an absolutely deserted forest make a sound?"

We also can ask, "If a communication is sent out and no one heeds it or understands it, has there actually been a communication?" The answer is that in the practical world of business no communication has taken place. Therefore, wise business communicators will always write with their readers' needs in mind. Unfortunately, however, when most businesspeople write, they are thinking only of themselves. What they write is usually a simple history of their own thoughts. They ignore their reader. They couldn't care less about their readers' needs and wants.

But you must care. And that care should reveal itself in every aspect of your writing: the message you send, whether you have written it correctly, how you have organized your thoughts, the words you have chosen, the sentence structure you have employed, the grammatical or punctuation mistakes you have tried to avoid, the inadvertently misspelled words. All of these factors have a decided impact upon your reader.

HOW READERS RESPOND

Throughout the last two chapters we talked about how you can engineer the impact of the message. We said that a high-impact message is one that is delivered to the reader in a clear, highly readable, right-to-the-point fashion. Its words leap off the page and demand that the reader examine them. A low-impact message is one that is obscured, roundabout, and buried under unnecessary words. Everything about the communication indicates that the reader would be better off ignoring it or throwing it away.

But what about the reader? What kind of emotional reaction will he or she give to certain messages? In a nutshell, readers experience one of three emotional reactions: positive, neutral, or negative.

Here's a message that elicits a positive reaction:

Dear Reader:

Congratulations! You have been selected from among thirty-five applicants for the position of regional personnel manager.

We will discuss the ramifications of this promotion at our next meeting. Let me indicate, however, that you can expect a 20 percent raise in salary.

"Terrific" says the reader, whose emotional reaction is one of joy and exhilaration.

But here's a message that evokes a neutral reaction, neither bad nor good.

Dear Reader:

We have received your request for the price of adopting our standard Series III Modulator. As soon as the cost information is gathered we will forward our price to you.

And here's a message that elicits a negative reaction:

Dear Reader:

We have discovered that you are responsible for the malfunction of our word processing equipment. Please see your supervisor, Ms. Smith, to find out where your errors occurred and to learn of the reprimands that are coming to you and your staff.

Reader reactions here? "Woe is me!"

FOUR READER RESPONSES TO A MESSAGE

What happens if we combine the impact the writer creates (i.e., high or low) with the reader's emotional reaction (positive or negative)? There are four possible combinations:*

1. High positive impact (HPI)
2. Low positive impact (LPI)
3. High negative impact (HNI)
4. Low negative impact (LNI)

These four responses give us a generalized terminology for discussion of business writing. Two of the four possible reactions

---

*If you think about it for a moment, you will agree that it is impossible to produce high or low neutral impacts. That just doesn't make sense. Neutral impact is neutral impact.

(high positive impact and low negative impact) are desirable under most circumstances, and two (low positive impact and high negative impact) are undesirable under most circumstances. Our job is to learn to engineer mechanics, word choice, sentence structure, and organization to create the desired effect.

A graphic description of these combinations will make the language even easier to understand and use. Look at figure 5–1.

Graphically, a totally negative or bad news message should be written so that it would fall at the lowest end (0–2) of the reader impact scale on the graph.

Conversely, a totally positive or good news message, if plotted on the graph, should fall at the highest end (8–10) of the reader

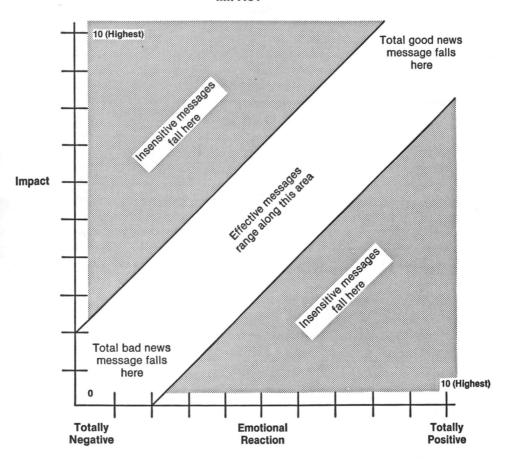

FIGURE 5–1.

impact scale. It is clear to see how problems will occur if a bad news message has high impact, for then its bad news is amplified and will undoubtedly anger and/or alienate the reader. And if a good news message has low impact, it thereby diminishes the effectiveness of the good news.

Effective messages will range along the unshaded area of the graph, depending upon their degree of positivity or negativity. The more positive a message, the more writers should use high-impact devices in their writing. The more negative a message, the more writers should avoid high impacting their words, sentences, and paragraphs.

Insensitive messages of both positive and negative nature will fall into the shaded areas of the graph.

Let's see how the language of high positive impact, low positive impact, high negative impact, and low negative impact works on actual messages.

> Your request for a larger office has been approved. You may move immediately to 31–B.

What kind of reaction does this elicit? Obviously, high positive impact. But what if this memo had been written as follows?

> After estimating our facilities' needs for the next five years, and projecting attrition of employees over the near term, it is evident that various persons may be eligible for facilities reassignments at times earlier than those originally projected. I am therefore pleased to be able to inform you that your request for a larger office has been considered and viewed affirmatively. You may, at your convenience, move into section 31–B.

This memo has low positive impact and would effectively undermine the response the writer desires. Instead of pleasing the reader, this memo would irritate her and probably encourage her to say, "Why in the world can't you ever tell me anything directly?"

LEARN TO ENGINEER YOUR WRITING

The truly sophisticated writer learns how to use writing as either an offensive or a defensive weapon. There are times when the writer wants a message to slash through the reader's consciousness and make a very strong, high positive impact on the reader. Mechanically correct, subject–verb–object simple sentences, along with Anglo-Saxon conversational words and a straightforward organizational pattern, will do just that.

However, there are other times when you may want to write something that does no more than simply lie there. Sometimes people are merely writing because they have to. The message is so basically negative that they have no hope of producing a favorable impression on the reader. All the writers hope for is that the message defends them from causing this reader to experience a highly negative reaction. In these instances, compound passive sentences, Latinate words, an indirect organizational pattern, and, in some instances, a dangling modifier or two are the weapons the writer wants to bring forth.

Which approach to use is up to you. But you now have the tools—word choice, sentence structure, and so on—and the language—high positive impact, low negative impact, and so on—to produce the effect you desire.

DR. JEKYLL AND MR. HYDE, OR HOW TO MAKE A SOW'S EAR OUT OF A SILK PURSE

The notion of engineering writing to achieve a desired effect is so important that we want to share with you one final dramatic example of how it can be done. The example, which we often use in our training sessions, is based on the premise that some people need to learn how to write poorly. We call this our Dr. Jekyll and Mr. Hyde exercise—the edifying example of a beautifully written, high-impact memo turning slowly but inexorably into a beastly communication almost too abhorrent to contemplate.

Here is the original memo, as sweet and pure a communication as was the scholarly and good Dr. Jekyll:

TO: J. D. Gibbons
       Director

FROM: L. M. Overstreet

I would like to exchange a few thoughts with you on the subject of interoffice systems. It is my opinion that:

1. While the systems have been around for four years, the definition, concept, and approach are still being developed.
2. People who have been involved in the systems have definite ideas on how management might "do it differently (better)" next time.
3. There is room for improved exchange of experiences from interoffice to external systems.
4. Installability, ease of use, human factors, and so on, are keys to our product's success, and a well-conducted evaluation is a vital assurance contribution.

To ensure continued success, let's consider and adapt to the above thoughts.

Note how this memo states the purpose clearly in the first sentence. Notice the highly readable, indented thoughts. We wish everyone wrote in such a high-impact fashion.

But wait! The potion has been administered, and Dr. Jekyll begins to change into the horrid Mr. Hyde.

First, he loses his itemization:

TO: J. D. Gibbons
       Director

FROM: L. M. Overstreet

I would like to exchange a few thoughts with you on the subject of interoffice systems.

It is my opinion that while the systems have been around for four years, the definition, concept, and approach are still being developed. People who have been involved in the systems have definite ideas on how management might "do it differently (better)" next time. There is room for improved exchange of experiences from interoffice to exernal systems. Installability, ease of use, human factors, and so on, are keys to our product's success, and a well-conducted evaluation is a vital assurance contribution.

To ensure continued success, let's consider and adapt to the above thoughts.

Then he changes from active to passive:

TO: J. D. Gibbons
       Director

FROM: L. M. Overstreet

A few thoughts could be exchanged on the subject of interoffice systems.

While the systems have been around for four years, in the still-being-developed stage are the definition, concept, and approach. Definite ideas on how management might "do it differently (better)" next time are held by people who have been involved in the systems. Room for improved exchange of experiences from interoffice to external systems has to be found. Keys to our product's success are thought to be installability, ease of use, human factors, and so on, and a vital assurance contribution could be a well-conducted evaluation.

To ensure continued success, adaptation to the above thoughts could be considered.

Next, his sentences lengthen grotesquely:

TO: J. D. Gibbons
       Director

FROM: L. M. Overstreet

A few thoughts could be exchanged on the subject of interoffice systems, for while the systems have been around for four years, still being developed are the definition, concept, and approach.

Definite ideas on how management might "do it differently (better)" next time are held by people who have been involved in the project, and room for improved exchange of experiences from interoffice to external systems has to be found. Keys to our product's success are thought to be installability, ease of use, human factors, and so on, and a vital assurance contribution could be a well-conducted evaluation; in fact, to ensure continued success, adaptation to the above thoughts could be considered.

Horrors! He now becomes all one paragraph:

TO: J. D. Gibbons
       Director

FROM: L. M. Overstreet

A few thoughts could be exchanged on the subject of interoffice systems. For while the systems have been around for four years, still being developed are the definition, concept, and approach. Definite ideas on how management might "do it differently (better)" next time are held by people who have been involved in the project, and room for improved exchange of experiences from interoffice to exernal systems has to be found. Keys to our product's success are thought to be installability, ease of use, human factors, and so on, and a vital assurance contribution could be a well-conducted evaluation; in fact, to ensure continued success, adaptation to the above thoughts could be considered.

Finally, and tragically, his statement of purpose falls off:

TO: J. D. Gibbons
        Director

FROM: L. M. Overstreet

While the systems have been around for four years, still being developed are the definition, concept, and approach. Definite ideas on how management might "do it differently (better)" next time are held by people who have been involved in the project, and room for improved exchange of experiences from interoffice to external systems has to be found. Keys to our product's success are thought to be installability, ease of use, human factors, and so on, and a vital assurance contribution could be a well-conducted evaluation; in fact, to ensure continued success, adaptation to the above thoughts could be considered.

There he stands, Mr. Hyde in all his appalling repulsiveness, mocking the world, daring readers to comprehend what he supposedly communicates. And yet, as repellent as they are, Mr. Hyde-like memos and letters are far more likely to be found in corporate files than are ones as beautiful and clear as those like the good Dr. Jekyll.

Fortunately, readers of this book have in their possession the antidote for Mr. Hyde letters. They know just what steps to take to restore such memos to their original Dr. Jekyll-like purity. They first replace the statement of purpose, then they return the paragraphs, shorten the sentences, return the active voice, replace the itemization, and, there once again, good as new, is Dr. Jekyll. (See pages 82 to 83.)

6

NOW IT'S UP TO YOU

The subject of the *Harvard Business Review* article that led many years later to this book came about by accident. One day a vice-president of a major corporation thundered red-faced into an office, shouting, "What do they mean I can't write?" When he had been sent to Harvard Business School's Advanced Management Program, this executive—whom we'll call Bill—felt sure he was being groomed for the senior vice-presidency he coveted. Instead, a rival had been appointed to the position. The CEO of Bill's company told him the reason for the negative decision. "Bill, you simply can't write!"

Bill sought counsel about his writing. "What do they mean I can't write?" he wanted to know. Was he really a poor writer? Bill considered himself very good. An examination of a week's worth of correspondence showed that Bill could write very well indeed, so well that, in fact, he seldom stopped. His memos, while beautifully written—sentence by sentence—were longwinded, rambling, and boring!

Bill's associates simply had to do too much work to wade through his daily torrent of six- and seven-page memos that said little or nothing. It got so bad that literally everyone refused to read them. For months—or even years—Bill worked hard every day creating volumes of memos destined for corporate wastebaskets.

Yet, as Bill put it later, with tears in his eyes, "Why didn't they tell me? I worked for that company for twenty-three years. Nobody ever said there was anything wrong with my writing!"

And that quite probably was true. Bill's superiors were too embarrassed to confront Bill with his problem. Furthermore, they were undoubtedly so uncertain about writing themselves that they weren't about to cast the first stone.

This type of foolish, wasteful, even ultimately cruel behavior must stop in companies. And stopping this behavior begins with you. For if you are not a manager now, there is no doubt you will be soon.

WRITING TO GET THE JOB DONE

This book and its checklist give you all the tools you need to demand—and obtain—effective business writing from yourself and from the people you manage. The checklist has been in use for many years. It works. Use it.

The very existence of the checklist makes it less embarrassing to discuss writing. It's impersonal. It helps you to criticize constructively those you work with. It frees you from setting yourself up as a judge and jury. You do not have to worry about whether you are a good enough writer to get away with it.

Arrange for regular writing review sessions with your colleagues. Make discussions of writing routine. Make effective writing important. Make it something everyone works toward. Focus on the positive, on becoming better. Soft-pedal harping, carping, and nitpicking. There is no one in the world whose writing cannot be criticized. Don't allow yourself to expect perfection from ordinary mortals. After all, *the object of business writing is to get the job done, not to create the perfect piece of prose!*

We have italicized this statement to emphasize its importance. Many highly intelligent, insightful people in our classes tell us that they are intimidated by the knowledge that they will never be truly fine writers. But to whom are they comparing themselves? Dickens? Hemingway? Updike? How fair is that?

And, to be really fair, just how good a business writer would the cerebral, poetic John Updike really be? Probably not so hot, because he would find it difficult, most likely, just to write to get a job done, instead of telling a story or creating beautiful language.

One woman in a class of ours told her fellow trainees that she was overjoyed by the discovery that beautiful writing might not actually be as effective in most business situations as plain, simple expression. She had brought in for class evaluation an extremely well-phrased letter her boss had written.

The class, however, not sharing her literary values, found the letter to be overwritten and pretentious. They didn't like it at all and felt that it simply was not well suited to the communication job at hand.

The class reaction served to free the trainee from apparently constant but subconscious criticism of herself for not being a fine literary stylist. She now recognized that she merely had to write in such a way as to accomplish whatever communication task she faced without causing unpleasant side effects. Forethought, honesty, simplicity, and sensitivity all ranked much higher than did stylistic felicity in business writing.

KNOW WHEN TO WRITE CORRECTLY

Remember that grammar, punctuation, and spelling mistakes cause more embarrassment than actual harm—most of the time! As the months go by, work with your associates to help each of you write correctly. Accept and believe the obvious, that after a while it will take all of you no longer to write correctly than it currently does to write incorrectly.

Grammar, punctuation, and spelling mistakes at the wrong time really can embarrass, because they reflect unfavorably on social class and educational background.

A middle-level manager was once so mortified that he was ready to jump out of his window. He had been having a running battle with his outer-office staff about punctuality—coming in late, leaving early, and taking longer coffee breaks than permitted. He wrote a tough memo and routed it with satisfaction through the office mail. That night a secretary circled in red in lipstick several grammatical mistakes, graded the memo "F" in two-inch crimson, and pinned it on the office bulletin board.

There's a lesson here. Not every communication needs to be carefully combed for mechanical errors. But those letters, reports, and memos that need it ought to get it, simply for your own protection.

We admit that for many memos flying around companies it matters little if they contain a mistake or two. But, on the other hand, writing correctly requires practice. If, in most of the routine writing you do, your company takes an "anything goes" attitude grammatically, then you won't be prepared to cope with that serious and important report prepared for the eyes of a key superior. You won't be in the habit of avoiding number and coherence mistakes.

The things you write are your calling cards. They represent you and reflect your knowledge and your educational background. Practice on the routine communications. Then you'll be ready for the truly important ones that can help or hurt your career.

SIX KEY ELEMENTS FOR SUCCESS

When you are judging the letters and memos you write, keep your focus on the truly important elements of effective business writing:

1. Are my facts accurate?
2. Have I answered all of my reader's questions?
3. Is the sensitivity of language and organization appropriate? Have I recognized that there's a reader out there with feelings and emotional needs almost exactly like my own?
4. Is the impact appropriate? Do negatives leap off the page at the reader? Bad! Do positives leap off? Good!
5. Have I chosen an appropriate organizational pattern to fit the type of communication? Or have I organized a negative letter like a yes-letter—or the reverse?
6. Have I recognized that even a supposedly informational letter frequently has to be organized like a persuasive letter? Do I appreciate that it is only by persuading readers to open up their minds to new information that the communication will prove effective?

These are the truly important aspects of effective writing; the aspects that differentiate communication from a mere relaying of data. Forgetting these points leads to serious trouble.

KNOW WHEN NOT TO WRITE

It always startles people when we say, "We don't trust writing!" But we really don't.

There are so many ways readers can distort what someone writes. "I was sorry to hear about your dissatisfaction with...." ("Oh," inteprets the angry reader, "you're not sorry I'm *dissatisfied.* You're just sorry to *hear* about it! In other words, why don't I just shut up!")

Or, "As I'm sure you'll agree...." ("How presumptuous," says the reader, "You're *sure* I agree, eh? Well, just for that, I don't!")

There are thousands of examples. Writing is at best inexact. But it is also one thing more. It's relatively permanent. It stays in the files for anyone to look at for years after you've written it. It doesn't go away.

If you and a colleague have a severe misunderstanding and exchange words in the privacy of an office, you have probably done little long-term harm. But if you both put your disagreements, countercharges, and accusations in writing:

- After amusing the word processing department, your bad words get spread all around the company.
- Your unfortunate memos stay in the files to cause future trouble.
- You both get permanent black eyes.

So ask yourself, "Does this memo or letter *need* to be written? Won't a phone call do as well? Is a personal visit better than even a good letter in a delicate, negative situation?"

But, above all, before you sign any letter, ask yourself, "Would I like to receive this letter?" If the answer is no, reject the letter and consider whether another medium, or another approach, isn't better.

PRINCIPLES OF EFFECTIVE BUSINESS WRITING

Principle 1: Something (a word or an idea) cannot be singular and plural at the same time. *Derived grammatical rule:* Number mistakes are violations of this principle. There are two types of number mistakes:

1. Pronoun and antecedent disagreement in number.
2. Subject and verb disagreement in number.

Principle 2: Ideas (or words) that relate to or influence the meaning of other ideas (or words) should be placed as close as possible to each other in a piece of writing. *Derived grammatical rule:* Coherence mistakes are violations of this principle. There are two types of coherence errors:

1. Misplaced modifier—a word or phrase (brick) illogically placed so as to modify (or influence the meaning of) the wrong word (or idea) in a sentence.
2. Dangling modifier—a word or phrase often ending with an *ing* word (participle) that modifies a word that is not in the sentence; hence, the brick dangles.

Principle 3: Never trust a pronoun. Avoid using pronouns as much as possible. Check those you must use for number and coherence.

Principle 4: An English reader's brain is programmed to believe that the noun nearest a pronoun and agreeing with it in gender and number is the antecedent of that pronoun.

Principle 5: Because a pronoun means nothing until a reader knows what noun it refers to, always put the noun first and then follow with the pronoun.

Principle 6: Readers' minds are programmed to receive language information in a subject–verb–object order. Put subject first, as much as possible, for high-impact sentences.

Principle 7: For sentences with high impact and high readability:
1. Use simple sentences as much as possible.
2. Try to avoid compound sentences.
3. Be selective in your use of complex sentences.

Principle 8: The passive voice drastically lowers impact. Use passive voice only when:
1. For diplomatic reasons you want to hide the subject from the reader.
2. You do not want negative ideas to leap off the page.

Principle 9: Readers don't like (or understand) many Latinate words; hooking Latinate words together creates gobbledygook.

Principle 10: Readers do like (and understand) most words from the Anglo-Saxon. Most conversation uses words derived from Anglo-Saxon.

Principle 11: If you write as you speak, and use the same Anglo-Saxon words, readers will understand you better.

Principle 12: For high-impact paragraphing:
1. Use short paragraphs. People find them more readable than long ones.
2. Itemize and indent multiple ideas in paragraphs.
3. Allow plenty of white space on the page. Readers unconsciously react favorably to it.

Principle 13: Determine whether your communication is positive or negative to the reader's interests *before* you write. If it is negative, organize your thoughts according to the no-letter formula. If it is positive, organize according to the yes-letter formula.

Principle 14: Organize a no-letter according to this formula:
1. Begin on a neutral note. Don't give false hope or mislead the reader. But don't throw a harpoon in the first paragraph.
2. Introduce the topic.
3. Educate the reader. Explain why. Give reasons underly-

ing the negative decision that follows.
4. Either say no or offer a substitute for no (such as, "If you improve in six months, we'll reconsider").
5. End on some pleasant or business-as-usual note.

Principle 15: Organize a yes-letter according to this formula:

1. Say yes immediately.
2. If you have any counterfavors to ask while the reader is euphoric, ask them. (But don't look tricky or begrudging!)

Principle 16: Organize a persuasive letter according to this formula:

1. Don't try to con your reader. State your request clearly and immediately.
2. Show why the action desired is in the reader's or the company's best interest. But don't sound like a huckster.
3. Convince the reader (by use of meaningful and honest evidence) that what you want is reasonable.
4. Take the order—specify how, when, and where the desired action should be taken.
5. Make the action required as simple as possible. ("Just initial a copy of this letter, send it back to me, and I'll place the order.")

Principle 17: Organize an information letter according to this formula:

1. Frankly tell your purpose in writing and why the information conveyed is important, unless, of course, the reason is obvious, such as when you are answering a question.
2. Tell the reason why he or she is being given the information. Is there anything the reader is supposed to do with it?
3. In other words, quickly persuade your busy reader that your message is worth reading.

APPENDIX B

USE COMMON SENSE TO PUNCTUATE

Punctuation was not invented just to cause trouble. It was invented to serve, like grammar, as an aid to understanding written language. Grammar is virtually completely logical. Punctuation is part logic and part convention. But whatever it is, punctuation is nothing to be afraid of, nor is it something difficult.

HOW SENTENCE CONSTRUCTION DETERMINES PUNCTUATION

Most punctuation problems begin to evaporate once you recognize that they exist only in relation to sentences you construct. It is your own fault if you write such complicated sentences that you can't punctuate them. Most of the terrible sentences you recall puzzling over in your grammar school workbooks did not need punctuation as much as they needed rewriting.

Some rules of punctuation related to sentence construction are outlined in this section. Once you have absorbed these rules, you will have learned 80 to 90 percent of all you need to know about practical, everyday punctuation. The key to the whole matter, of course, still depends largely on whether or not you know precisely what types of sentences you are writing.

There are only three types of sentences a sensible writer needs to compose: simple, compound, and complex. Once you learn how each of these is normally punctuated, you should have little trouble.

Therefore, we must make sure that you really understand what a sentence is. (We are not going to deal here with fragmentary conversational sentences like "Oh" or "So what?") A sentence is nothing more than one or more independent clauses, or a combination of one or more independent or one or more dependent clauses.

This business of clauses will seem much simpler if you remember the fifth-grade definition that a clause is a group of words containing a subject (the thing that acts or is acted upon) and a predicate (a description of the action). Clauses that can stand alone ("I get up in the morning") are independent. Clauses that cannot stand alone ("When I get up in the morning") are dependent.

When you get right down to it, an independent clause is a sentence, and a dependent clause is not a sentence. No matter how you punctuate a dependent clause, you can never make it a sentence. But for simple, compound, and complex sentences, the rules of punctuation are quite simple:

A. *Simple sentences* (one independent clause, one sentence): Anybody can punctuate these. You put a capital at the beginning and a period at the end.

B. *Compound sentences* (two independent clauses, hence two sentences): There are three ways a compound sentence can be punctuated.

   1. Insert a semicolon between the clauses. ("I get up in the morning; I brush my teeth.") This use of the semicolon is similar to that of a period.
   2. Insert a comma plus a coordinating conjunction (*and, or, but, nor,* or *for*) between the clauses. ("I get up in the morning, and I brush my teeth.") Many of us falsely regard *however, then, yet,* and *thus* as coordinating conjunctions and put commas before them when they separate two independent clauses. These words actually join nothing; thus (as in this very sentence), a semicolon is required before them.
   3. Insert a period between the two independent clauses and make two separate sentences. ("I get up in the morning. I brush my teeth.")

C. *Complex sentences* (one or more independent clauses plus one or more dependent clauses): Dependent clauses, since they cannot stand alone, must be attached to independent clauses in the following ways.

1. When the dependent clause comes first, set it off from the independent clause by a comma. ("When I get up in the morning, I brush my teeth.")

2. When the dependent clause comes after the independent clause:
   a. It is set off by a comma if the dependent clause is not absolutely necessary to the meaning of the independent clause.
   b. It is not set off by a comma if the dependent clause is necessary to the meaning of the independent clause.

   Take the simple example we have been using. ("I brush my teeth when I get up in the morning.") Here, the punctuation (the absence of the comma) shows that the dependent clause ("when I get up") is necessary to the meaning.

   In another example—"John won the race, although it was close"—the dependent clause is considered not necessary to the meaning and has been set off by a comma. Suppose, however, the example had read like this: "John won the race because he cheated." For the writer to put a comma before *because* would tell you that the following dependent clause is not necessary to the essential meaning of the main dependent clause. Obviously, though, it is necessary, since John won because he cheated. Thus, the writer has put no comma before *because*.

3. When the dependent clause falls in the middle of the sentence:
   a. It is set off by commas if it is not necessary to the essential meaning of the sentence.
   b. It is not set off by commas if it is necessary to the essential meaning of the sentence.

   Let us see how these rules work in practice. Here are some examples:

   "People *who live in glass houses* should not throw stones." The fact that the writer has not put commas around the italicized dependent clause shows that it is necessary to the essential meaning of the sentence. If the writer had put commas around the middle clause, the essential meaning of the sentence would be this: "People should not throw stones." Obviously, the real meaning of the sentence would have been lost if the writer had foolishly labeled the middle dependent clause as unnecessary.

   "All of my money *which I left on the beach* was stolen." In this case the correctness of the punctuation of the middle clause depends on the meaning intended by the writer. If the writer puts commas around the italicized clause, the statement means that all of the money (every bit of it, everywhere) was stolen. If this is what the writer means, fine. But if he or she means to tell us that only the money left on the beach was stolen, then the writer had better not take the middle clause out of the sentence by putting commas around it.

"The company office *which is located in Montreal* handled the job." What does the writer mean here? If the company has offices located in cities other than Montreal, the italicized clause is necessary and should not have commas around it. If the company has no other offices, then the italicized clause is not necessary and should have commas around it.

All of the sentences we write fall within these types. (If they do not, something is wrong!) Since we know how each of these should be punctuated, we should have little difficulty in punctuating most of what we write. We say most because there are a few more general rules on punctuation that should be covered.

HOW TO HANDLE PHRASES

Some of you may wonder at this point whether we have forgotten about phrases (groups of words not containing a subject and a predicate); certainly, these should not be overlooked. Here are some simplified but practical rules:

A. Any word or phrase that seems out of place in the normal order of the English sentence (subject–verb–object) can be correctly set off by commas.

1. Normal order: "I brush my teeth in the morning."
   Out of order: "In the morning, I brush my teeth."

2. Normal order: "XYZ is a management consulting firm which has an excellent reputation in New England."
   Out of order: In New England, XYZ is a management consulting firm which has an excellent reputation in New England."

3. Normal order: "XYZ is respected throughout New England for the high-quality consulting services it offers."
   Out of order: "Respected for the high-quality consulting services it offers, XYZ operates throughout New England."

4. Normal order: "Experts tell us that business is poor."
   Out of order: "Business, experts tell us, is poor."

5. Normal order: "I think business is poor."
   Out of order: "Business, I think, is poor."

B. Any word or phrase that is interjected into a sentence but is not absolutely necessary to its meaning is set off by commas.

1. "Business, alas, is terrible."
2. "Alas, business is terrible."

3. "To tell the truth, I am tired."

4. "Nothing, on the other hand, will prevent me from arriving on time."

5. "Nevertheless, I shall try."

6. "Mr. Brown has retired; nevertheless, he still retains considerable influence over the company." (The fact that *nevertheless* or other similar conjunctive adverbs like *however, therefore,* and so on, come at the beginning of a sentence should not make us regard them as pure conjunctions. Hence, the semicolon before *nevertheless* is used.

WHAT IS AN ELLIPSIS?

Occasionally you will come across three dots in the middle of a sentence. This means that words have been omitted from a statement that is being quoted. (A fourth dot at the end of a sentence merely stands for the period.)

1. Original: "At any specific point in time, including the time at which its management confronts a management problem, a business has a number of characteristics."

2. With omissions: "At any specific point...a business has a number of characteristics."

HOW TO DASH

The dash is used to indicate a sudden or unexpected shift in the flow of the statement or to heighten surprise. Dashes are also used to emphasize an appositive or to take the place of parentheses.

1. "Movies are better than ever—or so the press agents say!"

2. "Lyndon Johnson—our former president—was born in Texas."

3. "Patriots—and I trust we are all patriots at a time like this—will not hesitate to act."

HOW TO USE PARENTHESES

Parentheses are used 1) to enclose examples or parenthetical material, 2) to enclose material that is only loosely connected with the main thought of the sentence, and 3) to set off itemized numbers or letters—as in this sentence.

HOW TO PUNCTUATE ITEMS IN SERIES

1. If a sentence has one subject and two predicates, the predicates are not usually separated by a comma. ("John wrote his report and then went to bed.")
2. If a sentence has one subject and more than two predicates, the predicates are separated by commas. ("John wrote his report, went to bed, and woke refreshed.")
3. Rule 2 applies to items in series. Each should be separated from the others by a comma. ("John, Bill, and Jim all wrote reports on Tuesday night.")

HOW TO USE QUOTATION MARKS

All marks of punctuation (except the semicolon, colon, and, in special cases, the question mark and the exclamation point) go within quotation marks.

1. "What?" said the Controller, "I will not do it!"; then she strode from the conference room.
2. Is there such a word as "phooey"? (To put the question mark inside the quotation mark would signal that the mark refers to the word *phooey* and not to the entire sentence.)
3. Words like "patriotism," "democracy," and "free enterprise" are often employed for their effect.

HOW TO PUNCTUATE INDENTATIONS AND LISTS

Items in a list should be punctuated the same whether or not they are indented.

1. The company intends to: 1) obtain a larger share of the market, 2) increase profits, and 3) avoid unnecessary expense.
2. The company intends to:
   1) obtain a larger share of the market,
   2) increase profits, and
   3) avoid unnecessary expense.

WHEN TO USE BRACKETS

Brackets are used 1) to mark an interpolation added by the writer to material he or she is quoting, and 2) to enclose a parenthetical expression in a part of a sentence that is already enclosed by parentheses:

> The example he quoted (McNair's *The Case Method of Instruction* [3rd Edition]) contained the exact reference.

PRE-TEST ANSWERS

1. Lack of number agreement between subject and verb. (*List* is singular. *Are* is plural. Correct verb would be *is.*)
2. Lack of number agreement between pronoun *they* and its antecedent noun, *inventor.* (Correct pronoun should be *he* or *she.*)
3. Lack of number agreement between subject and verb. (The subject is *capabilities and resources;* therefore, the verb should be *are,* not *is.*)
4. Misplaced modifier. (*It* cannot *consider.* The *considering* phrase needs to be placed near the word in the sentence that does the considering, i.e., *we.*)
5. Vague pronoun. (What does *this* refer to?)
6. Lack of number agreement between subject and verb. (*The Dallas transportation department,* the subject following *nor* and hence the word that determines the number of the verb, is singular and thus requires a singular verb, *has,* not *have.*)
7. Misplaced modifier. (*ABCD* was *designed.* The *applications* were not designed.)
8. Dangling modifier. (There is no subject in this sentence that can be *setting the headcount requirements; it* certainly can't. Therefore, the phrase beginning with the participle *setting* dangles.)
9. Vague pronoun. (What does *these* refer to?)
10. Dangling modifier. (There is no subject in this sentence that can be *analyzing the data;* therefore, again, a participle phrase dangles.)

INDEX

NOTES

NOTES

NOTES

NOTES

NOTES

NOTES

NOTES

NOTES

NOTES

NOTES

NOTES

NOTES